MW00531951

A Journey for Two

A Journey for Two

Mother and Daughter Caregiving Relationships

Jeanne R. Lord

ROWMAN & LITTLEFIELD
Lanham • Boulder • New York • London

Published by Rowman & Littlefield
An imprint of The Rowman & Littlefield Publishing Group, Inc.
4501 Forbes Boulevard, Suite 200, Lanham, Maryland 20706
www.rowman.com

6 Tinworth Street, London SE11 5AL, United Kingdom

British Library Cataloguing in Publication Information Available

Library of Congress Cataloging-in-Publication Data

Names: Lord, Jeanne R., author.
Title: A journey for two : mother and daughter caregiving relationships /
    Jeanne R. Lord.
Description: Lanham : Rowman & Littlefield, [2021] | Includes
    bibliographical references and index. | Summary: "Explores the beautiful
    and complicated mother-daughter relationship in the context of
    caregiving for an ill or aging mother and offers tips and suggestions
    for overcoming the more difficult aspects while celebrating and
    cherishing the more comforting features"—Provided by publisher.
Identifiers: LCCN 2020056810 (print) | LCCN 2020056811 (ebook) | ISBN
    9781538152898 (cloth) | ISBN 9781538152904 (epub) Subjects: LCSH:
Aging parents—Care. | Mothers and daughters. | Adult
    children of aging parents. | Caregivers—Family relationships.
Classification: LCC HQ1063.6 .L67 2021 (print) | LCC HQ1063.6 (ebook) |
    DDC 306.874084/6—dc23
LC record available at https://lccn.loc.gov/2020056810
LC ebook record available at https://lccn.loc.gov/2020056811

For my mother, Sandra

Contents

Acknowledgments

It is a privilege to acknowledge and thank, with sincere appreciation, the ten families who so graciously gave of their time and allowed me to share in their lives. A special thank-you goes to Dr. Loretta Prater for her support and encouragement. I extend my respect and friendship to a brave, strong, and talented woman. A special note of thanks goes to Dr. Charlotte England for her early direction, guidance, and insights. Love and thanks goes to my son, Riley, and my daughter, Anna. They are a source of inspiration and a shining light in my life. A special tribute goes to my late grandmother, Eileen Welch, who served as the inspiration for the writing of this book. She died on the same day that I learned that this book would be accepted for publication. Eileen was ninety-nine and a half and was full of generosity and beauty. Her children, grandchildren, and great-children will never forget how their lives were changed by her love.

Preface

I'm afraid and I'm sad—afraid for what the future holds and sad for the changes time has brought us. Daily, I watch my mother struggle with caring for her mother, her best friend, a woman she always admired. It isn't that she thought her mother was perfect, and any negative behaviors are infrequent and overshadowed by her generosity, sense of humor, positive spirit, and beauty. Her mother is frail but in fairly good health at age ninety-nine and a half, despite the congestive heart failure that will eventually take her life. My mother doesn't really have to do any physical personal care tasks for her, and my grandmother certainly does not want anyone bathing her. She won't allow this, so she tries to keep herself clean. She does, however, need her meals prepared and medications monitored.

I mentioned my mother was struggling with providing care for her. It is the emotional support my mother must provide that is taking its toll, as well as the fact that my grandmother seems to be so angry and upset so much of the time, for no seemingly logical reason. My mother is hurt that her mother doesn't seem to appreciate that she is there each day, waiting on her, listening to her, loving her, bringing her good things to eat, offering up fun things they might do together, and willing to be best friends just like they used to be. My mother will say, "Mom, I am here, please just appreciate what we have together and the time we have left. Let's do something fun, like get in the car and go get some ice cream and then come back here and I will give you a pedicure." This is answered with tears, and that she doesn't feel like it, and if she goes, she might fall or faint. This is an everyday occurrence, and it never changes. She is receiving appropriate treatment for depression from her doctor, and any forms of dementia have been ruled out, as she is able to converse on current topics and write cohesive, one-page memories of her life and childhood.

It has taken all of us time to think through what is happening, but finally, we realize that she is grieving—grieving for her former life of when she was strong, capable, needed, and active. After all, at one time, when she was in her seventies, she served as the vice president of operations of a popular franchise and oversaw three stores in our area, and now she isn't even able to go outside to get the mail or barely leave the couch in the living room. She used to put her work clothes on each day, and her hair and makeup were perfect as she headed out the door to manage a large staff. On weekends, well into her early nineties, she was still using a riding lawn mower to take care of the yard. Of course, she is suffering a loss, and she is very angry about that and terribly sad. She is grieving the loss of her autonomy, the loss of being able to care for herself in the meticulous way that she was accustomed to doing, the loss of driving, and the loss of her beautifully decorated home, which she still lives in but, over the years, has deteriorated from lack of care.

My mother is grieving, too. She is grieving for her mother, her best friend and confidante, and the lost role of being the daughter. Every day, my mother tells me, "I am fine. I am not going to let all of this get to me." Her ongoing stomach issues and hair loss tell me otherwise. I offer my mother what I can at this point—lots of listening, encouragement that she is doing all the right things, some meals for her and my grandmother to enjoy together, and a reminder that she must set limits and boundaries and not overdo and over give, just because she thinks that is the way to be a good daughter. She still wonders why she is not enough to fulfill her mother's needs, to make her happy, to somehow make her better. Why is nothing she does ever enough? She wonders, "I have my mother, but do I really?"

Introduction

There are only four kinds of people in the world: those who have been caregivers, those who are currently caregivers, those who will be caregivers, and those who will need a caregiver.

—Former First Lady Rosalynn Carter

My mother was beautiful—always. Even in her forties she was a head-turner. She was blonde, dressed to the nines, had a great figure, and always smelled so good. Everyone loved her personality. My mother was easy to love, and I wanted to be with her, forever. In her fifties, she was beautiful and fun to be with, and her grandchildren loved being around her. I thought to myself, *I want to be with her, forever*. In her sixties, she got a face-lift to make sure she stayed beautiful. Her body still looked good, and on into her seventies, she was mowing the yard in her bathing suit, still blonde, tan, fun. My martini-drinking, beautiful mother—my hero—I could never let her go. I wanted to be with her, forever. In her eighties, I loved her so much—she was interesting, up on current events, still beautiful, still drinking martinis, and still driving. I told her, "Mother, you can never die, your grandchildren would be devastated." She looked thoughtful for a moment and said, "Well, we just won't tell them!" I thought, *She is going to live forever!* She is now ninety-nine—and she has been falling a lot, doesn't always look very fresh or put together, isn't much fun, isn't interested in current events, and is not very lovable most of the time. I was with her in the ER the other day, after she had fallen, to get her knee checked out. I was exhausted, both physically and mentally, from the extra care I had been providing and especially from the attention she seemed to be needing. The plan was to have her go for a few days to get physical therapy at an assisted living facility, and honestly, I was grateful to be getting a bit of a break. Then the nurse came in and said, "The plans have changed. You can take her home now, and we will send someone to the home to provide physical therapy." *Well*, I thought, *together, forever—not really how I imagined it would be.*

This excerpt is a personal reflection of my mother's, regarding my grandmother. What this book will set out to explore is the quality of the mother/daughter relationship and how history, past associations, attitudes, and experiences affect the perceptions of the care that daughters provide to their mothers and mothers' perceptions of the care they receive from their daughters. In several of the mother/daughter "stories," we get a three-generation perspective, whereby a child of the caregiving daughter shares their thoughts or the caregiver provides us with some insights into their child's relationship dynamic with their grandparent.

Along the way, as we take a close and very personal look into the lives of mothers and daughters and their caregiving relationships, you might read something that sounds familiar, contemplate what is unfamiliar, and/or learn something that may be of help in understanding the caregiving relationship that you are now experiencing or will be in the future—whether anticipated or unanticipated.

Because my mother almost always had a very close and loving relationship with her mother, the care she now provides is done with a sense of "Well, she deserves for me to be there for her. After all, she was there for me." However, it doesn't mean that, at times, my mother isn't completely exasperated with her mother. It isn't because she has to cook for her, or clean up after her, or coordinate trips to the doctor, or manage finances, or other kinds of essential caregiving tasks. The kinds of things that put my mother over the edge have to do with past behaviors and attitudes that would occasionally surface through the years when my grandmother felt that things were not going her way in life. For the most part, she was the amazing woman described earlier, but now in late life, with not much to do or focus on, the negative behaviors and attitudes that she, at times, could be prone to seem to be all that is left. My mother wonders, "Where are the other traits that I so loved about her?" And she says, "Thank goodness for the good memories of our past relationship that carry me through."

The other day, my grandmother was being particularly difficult—negative, frustrated, obstinate. So, my mother said, "Mom, how about a game today? I have written a word on each of these three pieces of paper. I will put them in this bowl, and you can choose one. Here is the thing, Mom. One of the pieces of paper says 'cry,' one says 'complain,' and the other says 'reminisce.' Listen, if you choose the one that says 'cry,' then that is what we have to do—both of us—and we really have to choose something to cry about. If you choose the one that says 'complain,' then that is what we have to do. We have to have a really good gripe session—about anything and everything—and just really let it all hang out. If you choose 'reminisce,' then we each get to share a memory that was important to each of us." Fortunately, her mother selected "reminisce." What my grandmother didn't know was that all three pieces of paper said "reminisce." I guess this is where you now have learned something about my mother's personality! They ended up having a wonderful afternoon of telling stories, sharing memories, and laughing!

MY RESEARCH

I interviewed eight adult daughters caring for their mothers, one daughter-in-law caring for her mother-in-law, and one niece caring for her aunt. This pair was very close and shared, what they described, as a mother/daughter-type relationship. All of the pairs had been involved in a caregiving/care-receiving shared-residence living situation for at least one year. Initially, I was concerned that I was intruding into the private lives of virtual strangers, but, on the whole, the interviews went extremely well. I was frequently impressed by the generosity of spirit and time they devoted to sitting down to what, at times, were several hours of interviews. I also appreciated the candor and, at times, vulnerability they showed when responding to so many of the personal questions I asked them during their separate and private interviews. The emotions expressed—anger, love, frustration, confusion, and pride coupled at times with tears, laughter, and smiles—further revealed the level of burden and satisfaction that the daughters and mothers were experiencing.

I recruited the mother/daughter dyads by first contacting social service agencies, churches, and adult day care facilities to assist in identifying adult daughters who were caring for their mothers in a shared-residence arrangement. In order to avoid violation of codes of confidentiality, the referring group or agency inquired among prospective participants and referred families who agreed to participate in the study. I was seeking households where the aging mother was cognitively capable of responding to interview questions but had physical impairments, which qualified them as a care-receiver. Additionally, I wanted to have a variety of types of households, so I first conducted a screening phone interview to ask questions regarding others living in the household, employment status of the daughter, and whether they had outside assistance or support. I then read a list of possible sources to determine the kinds of supports they used. I also asked the daughters to respond to a short questionnaire about the cognitive functioning level of their mother, along with questions about their mother's physical functioning level. If their mother needed assistance with three or more activities of daily living and were considered cognitively capable of being interviewed, they qualified for the study. At the end of the screening phone interview, I scheduled appointments for face-to-face interviews with the ten qualified families. I told the daughters that, to ensure confidentiality, all interviews must be conducted separately and privately. I assured interviewees that they could withdraw their participation at any time, that they were not obligated to answer questions if answering would make them feel uncomfortable, and that neither their names nor any other identifying information would be used in reports of the study. The names of all the participants in this study are fictitious in order to protect their privacy. All of the responses of the mothers and daughters are direct quotes.

Some of the key topics that you will read about as the chapters unfold include strained relationships, role reversal, commitment, lack of respect for differences, frustration, reciprocity, shared activities, conflict, and friendship.

The book is organized into fifteen chapters. The first five chapters compare and contrast the story of two mother/daughter pairs. The pairings serve as a basis for understanding the various differences in their perceptions, values, and attitudes that might otherwise have seemed inexplicable. For example, in chapter 1 the mothers in these two situations were quite similar in their physical and cognitive functioning, and yet the daughters' perceptions of their caregiving situations varied dramatically. Also, you will be able to fast forward to ten years later and have a look into the lives of the daughters, their perspectives (and how those may have changed), and what happened to their mothers. Now that it was ten years later, the mothers were either no longer living or were living in long-term care. These interviews ten years later revealed some surprising perspectives.

I have tremendous respect, admiration, and empathy for the caregiving daughters I interviewed. These women were trying to make sense out of a situation that most of them did not anticipate. A few of them had other dreams and plans. Interestingly, a couple of them needed their mothers, perhaps as much as their mothers needed them, but that meant that they had to face the inevitability of losing them and figure out how they would then accept this loss. Every caregiving daughter's situation was different; each provided care for their own reasons, and they each did the absolute best they could. Some had teenagers still living at home, some had unsupportive spouses, some still worked, and some had strained relationships. But every woman did her best, and that is all anyone could ask for in such a complex and intense situation. There are daughters, myself included, who have yet to face caring for their mother, and when the time comes for me, I hope I give my best. By the way, it doesn't mean that you won't get frustrated, feel angry or hurt, or feel guilty—it means you will hang in there despite all these things. Other people can offer up their advice and suggestions based on the information they have about your situation and based on their perception of your situation; but ultimately, other people truly have no idea what your life is like, and you just have to do what you think is right for you and your parent. As you read through the various chapters, I hope you can gain some insights from the various mother/daughter pairs and, in the later chapters, some ideas for navigating the complexities of caregiving.

Chapter One

Disapproval and Disappointment versus Appreciation and Respect

The mother/daughter pairs in these two households were similar in that both daughters were retired and each mother's physical and cognitive functioning were fairly high. However, the daughters were extremely different in their perceptions of their situations and life circumstances.

LILLIAN AND ELEANOR

Lillian

Lillian had been caring for her eighty-year-old mother, Eleanor, for roughly three years. Lillian was sixty years old, in very good health, married, and employed. Finances were not a problem in this household. Lillian's husband was somewhat helpful, but he did not like or get along with Eleanor. He was very unhappy with the shared living arrangement and was quite vocal about this.

Lillian cried throughout most of the interview, and I recall one particular moment when she became very emotional as she said, "It's difficult to become your parent. You see so much of yourself in your parent. It's terrifying. She doesn't say, 'Please' or 'Thank-you.' She says, 'I'll have.' I found myself doing that the other day, and [breaks down crying], well, I'm becoming just like her."

Lillian told me that she had not expected to become a caregiver to her mother. She said that the two of them had a history of a poor

7

relationship, which included poor communication and little affection. She described her mother as selfish, controlling, disruptive to the family, and unable to express affection. Lillian did not experience conflict with her mother, but she did experience a strained relationship, which had carried over from the past.

Lillian's husband had this to say, which added some insight into the relationship between Lillian and Eleanor: "We always have to keep her in mind for everything we do. Eleanor always has to make my wife feel as though she were secondary around here and that she is primary. I don't let Eleanor dictate anything I do."

Responses to the interview questions also demonstrated much of the emotional strain that Lillian was feeling: "None of the tasks are hard physically. It's mentally harder, especially diapering my mother or when we discuss past memories that my mother doesn't remember. We have never really talked about anything important. We've always had just superficial conversations. I wish she was more talkative about past things and present things" [becomes tearful].

The relationship between parent and child is probably the most emotionally powerful of all human relationships. Positive and negative emotions such as gratitude and love can mingle with feelings of frustration, anger, and resentment. Many studies and authors report that regardless of the strength of the emotional tie linking caregivers and care-receivers, some emotional stress is inevitable in caregiving. Caregivers may harbor feelings of exhaustion, discouragement, and isolation that seem relentless and overwhelming. Signs and symptoms that a caregiver is emotionally burdened may be subtle enough to escape the notice of family or professionals but significant enough to interfere with the caregiver's ability to meet role-related changes.[1]

Eleanor

During my interview with Lillian's mother, Eleanor, she was reluctant to answer questions in detail and was not highly verbal in her responses. She seemed very guarded, which was consistent with how Lillian had described her mother's reserved personality. Eleanor was eighty years old, had sufficient income to meet her needs, was fairly high in physical functioning, and had no problems with cognitive functioning. Her health condition included a heart problem and arthritis.

Lillian and Eleanor: Ten Years Later

Lillian took care of her mother for two more years after the time of the interview. She then made the decision to place her in a nursing home because of her declining cognitive functioning. Eleanor died two years later. Here is our interview:

Lillian: She had been in adult day care there [where she was placed]. My mother was in early Alzheimer's when you were here. She did real well, for some time. When she was in adult day care, the woman recommended she go into the Alzheimer's ward.

Jeanne: *Because she was showing symptoms?*

Lillian: Oh yes, she was not sleeping through the night; she was wandering. I was terrified, even though we had chains on the doors, so she really couldn't get out. I would hear her, so I would be up. So I wasn't sleeping well. And the one day I had got up, and she had dressed herself, so to speak, and had gone outside. She was not functioning very well. She still knew me; she never got mean like some Alzheimer's [sufferers]. She did really well. When she moved into the Alzheimer's ward she tried, and did very well. Then after she got diapered in the Alzheimer's unit she refused to walk. They have to be mobile. So they moved her into the regular nursing home. Although they took real good care of her, she didn't do so well. She was progressing in the disease. She got pneumonia, and they used to call it the "old man's friend" because she died in her sleep without going through any trauma. I knew my mother was in Alzheimer's. When we took her to the hospital with pneumonia, they asked us if we wanted them to give her any antibiotics, and we had not discussed it. But after a few hours, it was no big deal. I feel like my mother died much more in dignity if she had not had the antibiotics. She couldn't carry on a conversation, but she was still a person. By the time she died, she was a shell. That's what Alzheimer's does. It robs you of yourself. She was just no longer my mom. She didn't look good. She prided herself on her looks. She was a very dignified woman, and she was very beautiful. It is hard to watch yourself deteriorate. Putting her into a nursing home was a very hard decision.

Jeanne: *Why did you decide to stop care for her here?*

Lillian: I was still working; I had day help for her all the time. I think she enjoyed the day home while she was in the Alzheimer's unit. They kept them busy. It is the best nursing home in town as far as I'm concerned. And it was what I could afford. Mostly because I didn't think that I could take as good as care of her here. It was putting a strain on my husband, who was home all day; he was retired by then. It was hard for him to be here with her and a caretaker all day. And he is my first concern; it would make him upset. He is great with my mother. And my daughter was great with her.

Jeanne: *Did the quality of your relationship change in any way as your mother's health began to further deteriorate? If so, in what way?*

Lillian: No, I think we still had a good relationship while she was in the nursing home. I would come into the room, and she would say, "Oh, there's my daughter." I would sing songs to all these people. I would amuse these people for an hour or so. So, I think we still had a good relationship. My mother lived about three years too long, and it would have been better if she had died younger. She had a beautiful life, and we loved having her here; she loved being here. And she loved the grandkids. They would go to the nursing home with me. They enjoyed them.

Jeanne: *Did the quality of the relationship you shared with your mother help or hinder your decision to no longer provide care here?*

Lillian: It made it worse. I had not been home since I was seventeen. My sister had been in the city close to my mother. And my relationship, my mom and I had not been close; I left home at seventeen. My sister and she were very close. I think the time we spent together brought us close.

Jeanne: *So having to put her in a nursing home was very difficult?*

Lillian: Yeah, my sister had told me to do it way before.

Jeanne: *Was your mother helpful in making the decision? If so, in what way?*

Lillian: No, never protested. She never said anything. I think by that time, she didn't really realize what was going on. My mother never saved anything. She was not sentimental. So leaving her house, nothing really affected her. My father was very sentimental. My sister and I certainly take after him in that aspect. She had no sentimental things. She never kept papers, cards, anything like that. She never cried.

Jeanne: *In what way did the household functioning change as a result of the change in your mother's health and residence?*

Lillian: I didn't have to tell my husband to be nice. I knew he was not happy at that time. He put up with it.

Jeanne: *I remember at that time he said that because it was important to you, that is why he had her here.*

Lillian: Life was much easier after that. We could go and do more after that. It was not enough, but then he has his responsibilities. Now we have two cats. We didn't have to worry about going out at night. Easier, life was easier. We have more time, since I was there at least once every day.

Jeanne: *After the final transition was made, how did you feel?*

Lillian: You become the mother, the caregiver. My mother never gave support since the time I left home. I never lived at home with her. I lived two weeks with her between college and a summer job. I was home two weeks from the time I left home. I was young. My sister had been there a lot. After my father died, my sister fixed my mother up. My sister was the support person.

Jeanne: *Then you became the support person?*

Lillian: Yeah, yeah.

Jeanne: *Did you feel that old conflicts were resolved? Did new conflicts arise? If so, in what way?*

Lillian: I don't think so, no, no there were no conflicts between my mother and me. My mother and my husband, yes, there were conflicts. But not with my mother and me. I was really passive through the whole thing. And then I left, and then we never had conflicts.

Jeanne: *You never had conflicts while she was here?*

Lillian: No, she and I, no. And even she and my husband never had that bad of conflicts. I kept telling him it was not her fault.

Jeanne: *Was accepting your mother's death more difficult because of the relationship you shared?*

Lillian: As I said before, I think it was time. There were tears, and the usual mourning period. But I think it was time. My mother had a very good life. The end was not as it should have been. It was not as she would have wished. It was hard for me to see her that way.

Jeanne: *Did the fact that you did get along add to the grief of losing of her?*

Lillian: No, I think it was easier because I got to know her better, and I think we had a good relationship. It was easier because we got to connect and have that time.

Jeanne: *Was there a sense of loss, or was there a sense of relief after your mother's death?*

Lillian: Sense of loss and relief, both, and I think that is true when you lose an elderly parent.

Jeanne: *Do you feel that old conflicts were resolved? In what way? Did any new conflicts come about as your mother's health changed?*

Lillian: No, as I felt, we had no unresolved problems, and we didn't develop any. We had always gotten along.

Jeanne: *Looking back to ten years ago and thinking about now, has your perception of the caregiving situation changed in any way? If so, in what way?*

Lillian: I would do it all over again—if that's what you're asking. Absolutely, I would do it all over again. The only thing I would change is the pneumonia. I would have let my mother go. She knew that she was not herself. She was eighty-four when she died. And that is a good, long life. Now it doesn't seem so long in my perception now. I'm seventy-one, and eighty doesn't seem long. I have a lot of friends that are eighty.

Jeanne: *Looking back to ten years ago and thinking about now, has your perception of your relationship with your mother changed in any way? If so, in what way?*

Lillian: We always had a good relationship. I'm not sure she was always happy with me. But I was happy with her.

Jeanne: *I remember something you said ten years ago—that years ago, you weren't sure if she approved of your marriage.*

Lillian: She didn't, but I always thought that eventually she would. She would have liked me to stay in Chicago.

Jeanne: *That changed as you lived together?*

Lillian: Yes.

Jeanne: *Is there anything else you would like to add or that you think would be important for me to know?*

Lillian: I don't think you ever get over the death of a parent. But in the long run, it was not a real tragedy because we had something that lasted.

We will come back to Lillian and Eleanor at the end of the chapter to explore their caregiving situation. The next pair in this chapter is

Natalie and Hazel. Their caregiving situation was quite similar to the first pair. Both caregiving daughters were close in age and retired, and the care-receivers had fairly high physical and cognitive functioning; additionally, both caregiving daughters had some spousal support.

NATALIE AND HAZEL

Natalie

Natalie had been caring for her seventy-six-year-old mother, Hazel, for six years. Natalie was fifty-three years old, in very good health, married, and retired. Finances were not a problem in this household. Natalie's husband was very helpful to both his wife and to his mother-in-law and had an excellent relationship with Hazel. Natalie had a very good relationship with her mother, possessed a strong sense of family, and did her best to communicate with her mother, who had had a stroke and had some difficulty speaking. When I asked about their relationship, Natalie responded, "I mean, your mother is your mother. I mean it's nice to know she's there, and if you needed anything she'd stick up for you. It's hard to talk about and describe. If she's gone, I find myself walking in there to say hello, and it's like, oh yeah."

When I asked about caregiving tasks, she replied, "I mean you know it's just something that's gotta be done, that's all. I don't mind it [caregiving], I think there are times when I get disgusted and discouraged, and I think there are times I think you feel guilty like maybe you're not doing enough. I pretty much do what I want to do, you know, play golf, and I bowl, although it does limit you. It's stuff like running to town, for example, and that kind of thing. I probably don't do it as much as I probably would. We always want to include her; therefore, you do the things she can do, and you therefore are limited as to what you can do. It is just something that's gotta be done. You gotta do what you gotta do. Basically there are times when I resent some of the time I have to put into it. Overall [laughs], that's the way it is."

With regard to some of the emotional strain, Natalie had this to say: "It's always a combination of a lot of little things, you know. Like I said, she has a tendency to pout if something doesn't agree with her, and they add up. You know, it's like the straw that broke that camel's back, and you just go out and blow off steam and it's over. It's like a child again, and yet she's never gonna get any better; and with a child, you know they are gonna grow out of that stage."

Contributing to the positive relationship between Natalie and her mother were the shared activities that they enjoyed. These activities helped uplift them emotionally and gave them a sense of satisfaction.

"I enjoy taking her places she likes to go, like river boat gambling," Natalie continued. "She likes to play the slots. Making her stuff she likes to eat, buying her something that she likes. You feel like you're doing something to make her life a little easier, 'cause she's got it rough. It's very difficult to have to rely on your kids for everything. We like to go fishing together, go shopping, to shows, to eat, visit relatives, and take vacations. She's limited in what she can do. She doesn't like to get around a bunch of people, 'cause she feels more handicapped, I guess."

Natalie talked about deriving pleasure from making her mother things she likes to eat or buying her things she might enjoy. The concept of "uplifts" is very important to the process of giving care to a family member. Uplifts are small events that provide some response of pleasure, affirmation, or joy in the care-receiver and, ultimately, in the caregiver. The more uplifts in a daily caregiving situation can help the caregiver feel more satisfaction because it provides affirmation to the caregiver that they are doing things to bring about a positive experience for the care-receiver.[2]

Natalie and Hazel also enjoyed sharing a variety of activities together. One study examining mothers and daughters in caregiving situations found that daughters reported less burden and greater rewards if they participated in shared activities with their mother that were mutually beneficial.[3] Chapter 8 in this book takes a look at shared activities and offers up some ideas for you and your care-receiver. It is also important to remember that you, as the caregiver, have needs, in addition to the care-receiver, and that outside activities can play a role in providing a sense of well-being.

Hazel

Natalie's mother, Hazel, was seventy-six years old, had sufficient income to meet her needs, and had some very mild cognitive functioning difficulties that varied from day to day. She did have some health concerns, including a heart problem and emphysema. She also had a pace-maker, and she had suffered a stroke, which had caused some difficulty with her speech. She had short responses to the interview questions, but the answers below really highlight two things—that she does not like having to be dependent and that she, too, enjoys shared activities.

Hazel said, "I like to do things by myself, and I can't do them. I don't like depending on my family or anything, but I have to."

She continued, "We really like to go fishing, out to dinner, or shopping."

Natalie and Hazel: Ten Years Later

Natalie's mother, Hazel, was seventy-six years old at the time of our first interview. She lived to be eighty-seven and had just died within a year of the second interview. Natalie had cared for her mom a total of seventeen years. We spoke ten years later:

Natalie: In February we always go to Florida, and my brother always takes care of her. We had only been in Florida for one hour, and we got the phone call. She had had an ear infection, so we got her checked out and everything was fine. So it had to have been a stroke or heart attack. There is no way you could have known, you know. She died very peace-fully and fast. I don't think I could have ever put her in a nursing home. She couldn't walk, and she might have had to get in-home help. So it worked out the best for her. She didn't have to live in a nursing home or lay in bed. I wish I would have been there, but no I don't have any regrets. I often said that when she went it would be fast.

Jeanne: *Did the quality of your relationship change in any way as your mother's health began to further deteriorate? If so, in what way?*

Natalie: No really, the quality of the relationship would have been a lot better if she could have talked. At no time really while she was living here could she talk very well—she could communicate, but that was about it.

Jeanne: *Was accepting the death of your mother more difficult because of the relationship you shared?*

Natalie: It doesn't change my brother's life because he didn't see her that much, but it changes our life a lot. You know I don't know, I don't know. That's hard to answer. I got to say everything that I wanted to say, but I wish I could have gone back and had more patience with her. She always wanted to sit with me when it was the worst time. I had those feelings that I could have done more and could have done better. But then I think we did an awful lot, and that's just the way it is. I can't change that, if I'm not good at certain things. It is never easy to lose your mom. But I think I provided her with an awful lot. Even if we didn't agree on everything, she knew I was doing the best I could.

Jeanne: *Was there a sense of loss, or was there a sense of relief after your mother's death? If so, in what way?*

Natalie: Well, you know it hasn't been long enough. You know there was a sense of loss, but yet I know that it was only a matter of time before we had to make some changes. I didn't want to have to make those changes, so in that aspect it is a sense of relief. I'm not sure I could have made the changes to put her in a nursing home, because I know she would have hated it. She hates hospitals, and she hates doctors. Before I would have put her in a home, I would have taken her money to get some in-home care. Her mind was still good, so that would have made it even harder. The only time she would get confused was after the stroke—I would say something, and she wouldn't process it right and think I said something else.

Jeanne: *In what way did the household functioning change as the result of your mother's absence?*

Natalie: Well, I find myself getting her a glass for orange juice in the morning. And when I get home, I want to go in and check on her. We are a lot freer. She wouldn't be dressed all the time, but she got dressed for supper. We would get her ready and take her. But now we can just pick up and go. We are remodeling that room now, too.

Jeanne: *Do you think remodeling is good, or is it hard?*

Natalie: Yeah, I think it is helpful. I think that once we change it around I wouldn't expect to walk into the room to see her. And we got rid of a lot of stuff. You know it all went to family. It was something of Grandma's that they could use. I still—I am just automatic, I want to go in and check on her.

Jeanne: *Do you feel old conflicts were resolved? In what way? Did any new conflicts come about as your mother's health changed?*

Natalie: I really think the only conflict was her smoking. It was a big conflict. At the end of the day, if she had run out of cigarettes she would get mad at me because I wouldn't give her any more cigarettes. And then I would end up giving her one. We really didn't have any conflicts. There were times when I would be going places that I know she would want to go, but I was going with friends and I would not tell her where I was going. But I wouldn't really call that a conflict, but it could have been.

Jeanne: *Looking back to ten years ago and thinking about now, has your perception of the caregiving situation changed in any way? If so, in what way?*

Natalie: Probably not. I mean no, okay, not really. We became more limited in things we could do. We could have left Mother for a day. I couldn't go places after she got worse; the longest was three or four hours. She would go to bed about 7:00 p.m., so Wednesday night she could be alone when we went to play bingo. We just became more limited because she needed the care. I think my perception is probably the same. I just had to accept the way it is. And you go along and do the best that you can. I wish I could do this, and that was the way it was.

Jeanne: *Looking back to ten years ago and thinking about now, has your perception of your relationship with your mother changed in any way? If so, in what way?*

Natalie: Oh, I don't think so.

Jeanne: *Do you think the relationship you shared while giving care to your mother was similar to the one when you were growing up?*

Natalie: Well, it is more like I was the mother and she was the daughter. She was very self-sufficient. Feeling she was my mother, I still had that.

Jeanne: *Did she still try to be "the mother" when she was here?*

Natalie: I don't think so; Mother wasn't like that. I'm sure she told us what to do and how to do it. We were . . . it wasn't like . . . I don't know. Our family life was pretty easygoing. I decided I wanted to go to university, and that was it; there was no question. We were taught to be independent. I can't remember my parents trying to control my life, so it didn't happen now because it didn't happen then.

DISCUSSION OF INITIAL INTERVIEWS

Many of the statements made by the two daughters, Lillian and Natalie, indicate the variation in relationship quality and emotional strain. Natalie appeared to have less conflicted feelings toward her mother than did Lillian. Even though Eleanor's and Hazel's health conditions were somewhat similar, Natalie was able to interact with her mother by sharing and enjoying more activities. However, it is important to note that Lillian had to diaper her mother, which she found to be extremely upsetting. It appears that Natalie was determined to accept the situation and make the most of it, while Lillian was emotionally drained and yearned to have the kind of relationship with her mother that she had always hoped to have. Lillian confided in me, after the interview, that her mother never told her she was pretty, never approved of her marriage, and had always been terribly selfish. It appears that the burden Lillian experienced was not solely the result of caring for her mother but partly a result of a history of a poor relationship between the two. (Note: Eleanor went to adult day care during the day, so Lillian was not overly burdened by the physical tasks of providing care.) I have tremendous empathy for Lillian. She struggled with an unsupportive husband and an emotionally unavailable mother, but she gave her best and tried to connect with her mother.

Natalie had physical and emotional support from her husband, who also shared a caring relationship with Natalie's mother, Hazel. He would often communicate with Hazel when she would become frustrated about her speech problem, or he would build or fix anything on her side of the house that she wanted or needed. Lillian's husband despised his mother-in-law and always had. He admitted that he sometimes tried to be of help to his wife, but he would not lift a finger to assist his mother-in-law. He said, "Unfortunately, I'm around here for a few hours a day with her; I try to keep it to a minimum. I try to be outside while she's inside. She always tries to irritate me."

Neither Lillian nor Natalie were physically affectionate with their mothers, but Natalie had a stronger sense of family and feelings of closeness with her mother. Lillian yearned for a feeling of closeness, especially now that her mother was older, but was unable to achieve it since her mother was not emotionally available to her. Natalie indicated that her mother tried to help out and contributed to the household, whereas Lillian said her mother never assisted with household tasks. With Lillian and Eleanor, there was a history of a poor relationship, lack of spousal support, little reciprocity, and few shared activities. However, Natalie's responses indicated a high-quality relationship, spousal support, reciprocity, and shared activities. Natalie's responses to the interview questions revealed that she experienced less burden and felt more positive about the caregiving situation than did Lillian.

The interviews with both of the mothers, Eleanor and Hazel, were difficult. Eleanor was withdrawn and did not want to discuss anything personal, and Hazel had some difficulty speaking as a result of a stroke. The interviewing process required much rapport building with Eleanor and lots of patience with Hazel. Lack of privacy, loneliness, and dissatisfaction with care were not significant concerns for either Eleanor or Hazel. Hazel contributed to household functioning and was close to both her daughter and son-in-law. She also participated in a variety of activities with the family. Eleanor did not contribute at all to the household functioning, did not get along with her son-in-law, and was not a participant in family activities. She remained detached throughout the interview. Lillian indicated that this was very typical of her mother. However, Hazel was very warm and open and did her best to express herself.

It appears that the poor relationship between Lillian and Eleanor and the outright animosity Lillian's husband exhibited toward Eleanor resulted in mother and daughter being burdensome to each other simply by existing in shared space. Although Lillian said that caring for her mother made her feel good and that she owed her mother kindness and respect, these sentiments were not translated into specific attitudes and actions. They did not determine the atmosphere of the household. Lillian's specific comments about her mother conveyed a tone of distance, disapproval, and disappointment in the degree of helpfulness and companionship that she received from her mother.

Natalie and her husband had foreseen their role as caregivers and had prepared by modifying their home. Consciously or unconsciously, they had undergone a process of mental and emotional preparation, which is in contrast with Lillian's stark statement that she had not expected to become a caregiver. The kindness and respect shown by Natalie and her husband and the satisfaction they got from sharing this part of their lives with Hazel were made evident when their sense of limitations placed on them came not from the obstacle of her mere presence and demands of her needs but, instead, from the inconveniences encountered in connection with including her in a great variety of activities. By taking Hazel out to dinner, to shows, visiting, shopping, fishing, and on vacation, Natalie and her husband demonstrated and maintained their good relationship with her and with each other. Their cooperativeness and strong sense of family, and their consideration of Hazel's psychological and physical well-being contributed to their positive relationship. Because they saw her not as an invasive burden but rather as a family member who needed their help and could appreciate what they shared with her, much of what could have been a burden was transformed into satisfaction with successful management of some of the inconveniences of family life. Undoubtedly, if the atmosphere of the two households and the attitudes and values of the daughters and mothers had been more similar, the degree of burden Natalie felt would have been at least as great as that felt by Lillian because Natalie's mother actually had more physical problems than did Lillian's mother.

After the interviews with each household, I made note of my observations. I came to understand Lillian's tears throughout the interview, as well as her disappointment, and, unfortunately, I saw and heard her mother's disapproval. I also observed Natalie and Hazel's mutual, mother/daughter appreciation and respect.

Chapter Two

Self-focused Thinking versus Selfless Concern

The mother/daughter pairs in these two households were similar in that finances were not a problem and there were other family members in the house who provided some support. The main difference was the physical and cognitive functioning level of the aging mothers, which created very different reactions in the daughters in each of the households, but in very unexpected and surprising ways.

JANICE AND AMELIA

Janice

Janice had been caring for her seventy-eight-year-old mother, Amelia, for one year. Janice was forty-five years old, married, and employed part-time. During our conversations, she reported that she and her mother had a history of a low-quality relationship, which had been exacerbated by her mother's depression and emotional problems. The mother/daughter pair had little communication and gave no indication of affection. Similar to Lillian in chapter 1, Janice described her mother as being selfish and controlling. Janice's husband and teenage daughter were of little to no assistance and did not have a good relationship with Amelia; however, her two sons (age eighteen and twenty) in the household did try to be helpful and seemed to be quite understanding of the situation. Finances were not a problem in this household. Janice's father was in a nursing home.

During the interview, Janice was able to articulately verbalize her thoughts and feelings about caring for her mother and her relationship with her mother. She had this to say when I asked her if she had expected to become a caregiver to her mother:

"You never know how it's going to be. I used to dream that my parents would live here when they both were still well. Yes, I guess it is different. I expected a parent to move in being normal . . . still having all the faculties, and that's not how it was—is. Well, [maybe I could handle her being] physically ill, but not mentally, and that's been not what I expected. And now the reality of life and growing old has hit us all. It's affected my perspective, and I think I can say even our kids—their perspective on what it is to grow old. Just to grow old and look old is one thing, but to have your faculties taken from you, your independence, the knowledge of what's happening to you and the inability to do anything about it, it's scary, and I see firsthand now. We all see it and feel it, and then you've lost your parent basically. They're living, but they're gone."

What Janice describes about what she expected versus the reality of care is common, and frequently adult children have a persistent image of their parents as being impervious to harm and illness. They "forget" that their parents are growing old and need assistance, especially from them. Once realized, this discrepancy with reality results in feelings of stress and anxiety.[1] Particularly challenging for Janice, in this case, was her mother's moods. This caused a considerable amount of emotional strain for Janice.

"Nothing is hard, the only time it seems hard is when her mood becomes extreme. A depressed mood is very difficult. The paranoia is difficult. The angry mood is difficult. The good times she becomes extremely talkative, and that sometimes is hard to take. I, in one sense, feel like I'm repaying her for all the years of having the attention I got. On the other hand, I've become, because I'm the closest to her, the object of her anger. I'm the blame for her problems, the reason for her being here; [she's thinking] if only she didn't live here, everything would be okay; so I'm the target and the victim. I know deep down I feel like I feel good that I'm doing the right things. There are times I lose my patience and get snippy, and then I feel very angry at myself and her."

Janice went on to say, "I find myself trying to remember how she was, and that's hard to do sometimes. Just emotionally, just knowing she's not the person she was. I can't go to her. I can't get the emotional feedback from her that I need, and her mood is so negative and so nasty so much of the time. That's definitely become a real problem. It's hard to take that downer all the time. When she is in a really extremely depressed sort of angry, overtly angry state, which comes and goes, there's no telling when the mood swings will occur—those are the days that are very hard."

Another very challenging issue that occurs in caregiving, particularly in shared-residence caregiving is the issue of conflict between mother and daughter. Shared-residence caregiving can be a more intense situation since it involves more time spent together. If there are unresolved issues, then it may be harder to avoid the accompanying conflict that may arise. Janice had this to say:

"I was able to let things pass, and I thought I had resolved whatever conflicts we had until she came to live with me; and then they popped back up again, because the relationship is not stagnant anymore. It's dynamic again, and on a day-to-day basis, we have the same kind of encounters that we probably had when I was a child growing up. But I'm not the child anymore. In fact, I'm the parent now, to my parents. We've had a role reversal, and I'm not the same person."

Janice mentioned role reversal in her response. Oftentimes daughters who are caring for their aging mothers will feel as if they have now become the mother and their mother has become the daughter. In my own experience, I have noticed that my grandmother will sometimes say to my mother, "I've been a good daughter to you." Or "You are a good mother." She is confused about the relationship, since she definitely feels the role reversal that has taken place, even though she does not have dementia.

Janice had more to say about role reversal: "As a result of the illness, like I say, we've had a role reversal. That was the biggest change in our relationship. We go back and forth between whose house it is. I have the right not to listen to her, and I guess I feel angry at myself when I listen and respond and there's nothing to respond. If she were well, I could justify being angry and nasty much more."

As we can see from many of these quotes, oftentimes it isn't the amount of care involved and the level of assistance required by the care-receiver, it is the degree of disruption of the household functioning that creates instability in the house and in the relationship.[2] A quote from Janice's twenty-year-old son sums this up perfectly: "I can't say I'm ecstatic. She's with us, but it hasn't been the most pleasant of journeys to get to this point, and she's not the same lady. Of course, she's changed significantly from the grandmother I used to know. When things are very tense, it causes—the family structure just went. Everything that she is involved with is very tense. That includes eating dinner, getting up in the morning, going to bed, and everything in between. It changes not what you do, but how you relate to what you are doing."

I asked Janice if there were times that she felt close to her mother and she had this to say: "I feel close to my mother when she responds back. One night she sat on the edge of the bed and gave me a back massage like when I was a child. It just hadn't happened in all these months, and it may never happen again; but at that moment I felt very, very close. She was the giver and I was the receiver, and that felt really nice."

This was definitely a wonderful opportunity for mother and daughter to connect. Shared-residence caregiving can also offer up these kinds of moments for connection and reflection.

Janice not only had a twenty-year-old son but also a very wise eighteen-year-old son who had this to say when asked about things that can contribute to feelings of satisfaction: "That's very strange, burdens and satisfactions, some things can be both a burden and satisfying, especially looking back on something you did that was a burden. I didn't want to take her for a twenty-minute walk to listen to stories, but looking back I feel good about doing it. I should do it more."

He also had this to add about the overall situation: "Here she has her own room and her own family, but it's also a very bad thing. Her daughter used to live at her house. Now she lives in her daughter's house. She's a visitor. She doesn't want to feel a part of the family, but on the other hand, she is a part of the family, and she does, and so it's both. On the other hand, it's only temporary. It's not going to be for the rest of *my* life. When she passes away, I don't want to have any guilt feelings for not doing my share."

Amelia

Janice's mother Amelia was seventy-eight years old and had sufficient income to meet her needs. She was high functioning, physically, but had some cognitive functioning issues, which varied from day to day, primarily involving struggles with depression and mood swings. The twenty-year-old son in the household confided in me that his grandmother had tried a couple of times to commit suicide. She was aware that her husband was in a nursing home, but she did not talk about it. Her family indicated that she really didn't appear to want to visit him, but they coax her into going. A mental health worker visited her once a month to monitor her emotional status and her medications. Her responses to the interview questions primarily showed that Amelia really struggled with feeling her loss of freedom and feeling that she was a burden to certain members of the family.

"Well, for instance, music," Amelia said. "I have the love of music, but I don't feel free to play it when my family is home. It bothers me not being able to drive. I'm used to spending time alone, and I would prefer that. Being in the mood I've been in, there are times my daughter will set up an appointment for me; and then being in not a happy frame of mind, I won't want to go. Like a little child, I realize that. I know she feels bad about that."

Amelia continued, "She's always been a good daughter. It's hard to say. Oh, If we've had a few words or something and then we kind of get over it, and feel a little uh, you know . . . this isn't easy, I mean trying to relate all of this to you. Well, they're all very nice with the exception of the one I mentioned [granddaughter]. I just feel . . . I think she'd be better off not having me around. I try not to say or do anything to upset her [granddaughter]."

Janice and Amelia: Ten Years Later

Janice's mother Amelia only lived with her for a total of a year and a half. Janice made the decision to place her mother in long-term care.

Janice: My mother and I were very close and I am an only child. As a result of that relationship, having my mother, I know everything about my mother, the songs she liked, the food she liked, the clothes she liked. I was able to call upon her joys and needs in her background and could use that as a way to get into her head as she was getting to a point of serious deterioration. Once you live together and have a relationship where daughter is becoming mother and mother becoming child, so to speak, and the person who is ill does things because they are in pain, physical pain, or mental pain, that tests the relationship during that time. So it's not that we didn't get along during that time, I was just learning what it meant to venture, to recognize that when she would yell or scream or say things during this time, it wasn't her talking—but the illness talking. So, I find that the relationship wasn't closing, that the insight, that I brought, that helped me to evaluate it. The past history, what we brought up to that point that made the difference.

Jeanne: *How long after the interview, ten years ago, did you continue caring for your mother here in your home?*

Janice: During the year and a half my mother spent with us, she was admitted twice into the mental ward, and you know, I knew she was suffering from depression, and how much that was prior, it's hard to say, and that is how she ultimately went into the nursing home. She had to stay in the hospital; in fact, they almost didn't take her into the nursing home because she was so unstable. Of course, if they didn't take her, where would she go? Because there are no mental hospitals anymore. But in the end, she was taken in. During the year and a half she lived with us, she was going to the nursing home to visit my father. He had a stroke; he couldn't talk anymore but could still understand everything. My father's stroke is what really brought my mom down. Her symptoms of depression, prior to [the stroke], but this is the straw that broke the camel's back. So she would go to visit him and spend her days there.

Jeanne: *Why did you decide to stop caring for her here?*

Janice: Then when it was time for her to go in, it was clear she couldn't stay here anymore. She needed more care; it would have been such a hard thing. It was hard to have home health care. There are some kinds of problems especially with children in the home that are just impossible. There wasn't room for her; the hospital tried to keep her extra, so as to buy me some time, hoping they could find some room for her. There was nothing local. I was ready to die at the thought of having one parent here, one parent there, and they couldn't see each other. At the last second, something opened up, that they were going to discharge my mother that afternoon. They were together then another three years at the nursing home before my father died.

Jeanne: *How was the decision made to have your mother cared for elsewhere? How did you decide where?*

Janice: Mother was much more far-gone than my father. Eleven years later she knows me and knows I am her daughter. She has been wheelchair bound for eight or nine years. Everything just sort of went; she fell after the first year. She started out in assisted living. We knew her gait was deteriorating—she was a walking accident. She fell against the nurses' station and dislocated her shoulder. Then she was put in her wheelchair until she recuperated. But she never got out of the wheelchair. Never learned from the time she got in the wheelchair to even wheel it to make it go—she just smiled. Totally incapacitated. Today she sits in the chair. If you were to see her you would think she is totally okay, but her body—her legs are completely stiff as a board. Can't move her body at all. She can move her hands, but even now her right hand is very stiff and unable to open. She is unable to dress herself or feed herself. There will be a smile or laugh. I brought a friend to sing some songs for her.

Jeanne: *Did the quality of your relationship change in any way as your mother's health began to further deteriorate? If so, in what way?*

Janice: Mood swings is where it all began. I think what we don't know is nobody knows how to tell you—the thing that when most children find that their parent has Alzheimer's, they start to get annoyed and they don't realize that they are suffering from a disease.

Jeanne: *You had said that she wanted to maintain her appearance and how she looked?*

Janice: She has always taken pride in what she looked like and how she was dressed. My mother was always beautiful. I'll know she has really lost it when it doesn't matter to her anymore. The first thing I do when I go to visit is make sure her teeth are in her mouth and her glasses are clean. I put her in front of the mirror so she can look at herself, and it used to be that she would look at herself and fix her hair. But now she is totally . . . she doesn't even talk. And once in a while she will make an appropriate comment, but she generally can't follow a conversation. I go at least five days a week. I always allow myself at least one day a week not to go, and I always plan it at least a day before and I can look forward to it. It is part of my everyday life, and it's sometimes hard to go because I never know what I am going to find. I feel better after I have been there. It is a satisfying feeling. I expected more from my children than I did from my husband. [These were] their grandparents. I had to tell myself it was my responsibility and no one else had to help, but from the kids' eyes I talked to them a lot and I needed them to do some things and for them to go and talk and help. And I pushed them to it. And they did that. And when they came home [from college], they still would go visit. The time with Grandmother was important. Maybe she feels better and the eighteen-year-old son feels better after he has visited. And he is glad he did it. They learned compassion. I know it is hard for my husband.

Jeanne: *Did the quality of the relationship you shared with your mother help or hinder your decision to no longer provide care here?*

Janice: She began to ask her grandchildren to—she would be vocal, and ask to be driven to the store and buy pills. And at the end she just got progressively worse. She went into the hospital, once in March and once in July. I think it was a year apart. She would ask for the rides shortly after we went to see her. And then in June or July she was hospitalized for several weeks. We thought she almost died, partly because one of the doctors on the floor said to stop feeding her.

Jeanne: *She got worse both cognitively and physically?*

Janice: No, I would help her. In the beginning, she could shower and then she couldn't shower alone, and I think I began to put her in the bathtub. She couldn't even bathe with my help. I had a system; we would get up on our hands and knees, and she could eventually get up. I think the physical is related to the cognitive. Parts of the brain are dying. So obviously, part of it is controlling the physical parameters. And then in the beginning she could fix food for herself or fix a cup of coffee, and then that became too difficult for her. I put on a smile and go on with the day.

Jeanne: *That must be hard because it is easy to fall back into childhood ways. Things we grew up with, even if we know we don't want to do that.*

Janice: There were times, when very ugly, hurtful things would come out of her mouth, but I would get annoyed sometimes with hearing it. But I never believed or felt it was directed at me. Today I know they [her parents] are thrilled when I come, because I can get her to smile, eat, when no one is there. I have a great power with my mother, that she still knows me that's why it's not Alzheimer's. Great rewards from my mother. She will respond to me. I will take her arms and place them around me and say, "Oh, give me a hug." And she would respond. I believe that physical contact is so important, because there she doesn't get that. I couldn't get that from my mother, things I needed anymore as a child. But then I stopped expecting it.

Jeanne: *Was your mother helpful in making the decision to transition to a nursing home? If so, in what way?*

Janice: I have a master's degree in gerontology, and I remember as an undergraduate working in a nursing home. And I remember telling my parents I would never put them in a nursing home. I saw all kinds of problems. My situation was such that I couldn't care for them. My mother's condition was such that she was hospitalized for several weeks prior to the nursing home. It was beyond being at home at that point. I didn't know what was going to happen. And having my father already in the nursing home, I know what the nursing home was. I had established a relationship, my parents would be seeing one another, and it was time. My intention was to put her in her own apartment when my father had his stroke. She was just supposed to stay with us for a few weeks, and [she] became so weird in such a short time, that she had to stay with us, in a year and a half.

Jeanne: *Was she helpful in making the decision?*

Janice: No, she was out of it. Her behavior was so weird. She would have never made the decision. She had reached a point where she couldn't object. She was just not with it enough to make the decision. There was just no other way. She had spent several weeks in the hospital. And in the beginning, the day she got out before she went to the nursing home, it was my parents' anniversary. The cousins all came to help her move in. We did a party, and my mother knew who everyone was. She did for a long time know who everyone was. She has been there so long that her deteriorations has been going on for so long. The sicker she became the easier the decision was to have her in a nursing home.

Jeanne: *In what way did the household functioning change as the result of the change in your mother's health and residence?*

Janice: It was much better; we were already going to visit my father in the home, so now we just went to visit them both. It allowed me and my children to not have to see this on a daily basis, in our home. It allowed me to have a relationship with my daughter that didn't have my mother in it.

Jeanne: *I recall, your daughter was fifteen at the time and having a hard time with having your mother here.*

Janice: She was aware of my daughter and how she was feeling. My mother didn't want to socialize and didn't want to eat and come to the table. My daughter became this way.

Jeanne: *After the final transition was made, how did you feel?*

Janice: I am an only child, and I had a close relationship with my parents. I had been blessed with the chance to pay my parents back, and I know my father understood. I don't think my mother has the mental ability to understand. When mother dies, I will mourn her death, but I will have years to get used to it and know I have done what I can do. That I have given them—I feel lucky that we have been able to be part of each other's lives at this close proximity. I wish they were here and could see all the wonderful things. I feel like they know that things are on the right track.

Jeanne: *Do you feel old conflicts were resolved? Did new conflicts arise? If so, in what way?*

Janice: Yes, I felt that now I could, yes it was a sense of relief. And now I knew someone could take care of her. It felt like things were in place. Things only go right when I make sure they go right. There was a sense of closure.

Jeanne: *You had mentioned conflicts in the past. Did you feel any old conflicts were resolved?*

Janice: No, there were no conflicts. The only conflict was watching the illness take place. Learning how to live with her position and my new position.

Jeanne: *Looking back to ten years ago and thinking about now, has your perception of the caregiving situation changed in any way? If so, in what way?*

Janice: No, I was pretty aware of what was going on, and I don't think things have changed. I would do it again, yeah. I never regretted it. The only thing I didn't get about my father that my mother didn't see is that he was the one who was initially gone. And no one could understand me bringing my mother to live with me instead of having her living in Dallas, where I couldn't take care of her or my father, and I would have to go visit them. I know I made the right decision then, and I would advise anyone I know to do the same thing. If I tried to deal with my parents myself, it would have never worked. I hope professionals decide to do it this way.

Jeanne: *Looking back to ten years ago and thinking about now, has your perception of your relationship with your mother changed in any way? If so, in what way?*

Janice: My mother gave me what she could give me—what she could give me at the time. I think the biggest change has been that I can turn around and give back to her, and we—I guess I'm really lucky—we must have had a close relationship because I can go there and leave with smiles on my face. . . . I have no anger; I have sadness for the pain my mother has experienced. But when I get her to smile and laugh it just makes my day. When I don't go one day during the week, the next day I can't go soon enough. Visits don't have to be long; I have to make sure she is okay. There is something and always a challenge.

Our next mother/daughter pair in this chapter are Lois and her mother, Clara. Lois and Clara's situation differs from Janice and Amelia's because of the mothers' extremely different levels of physical and cognitive functioning and the daughters' very different perceptions of emotional strain and satisfaction.

LOIS AND CLARA

Lois

Lois was a retired, widowed, 81-year-old daughter, who had been caring for her 104-year-old mother, Clara, for one year. Lois's sister and her brother-in-law also lived in the house and assisted with the care. Along with being bedridden, Clara was, at times, incoherent and unable to interact with the family. Lois was a retired nurse and was proud that she had the nursing skills to care for her mother. Finances were not a problem in this household.

In the following interview quotes, Lois talks about being a retired nurse and understanding the expectations brought on by caregiving. She also talks about her sense of obligation and duty, not just as a daughter but also as a nurse, and that she puts the nursing part as her first priority.

Lois began, "I'm an old RN [registered nurse], and I happened to know what it [caregiving] would be. It isn't any different than I expected it to be. If I weren't caregiving, I would be working at Meals on Wheels and doing things in church, doing a little fooling around with the weeds in the garden, contending with the neighbor kids and the dogs, what anybody else does that lives so long."

Findings from other studies suggest that it is the characteristics of the caregiving situation and the resources available to the caregiver, rather than the direct condition of the care-receiver, that most directly affect the caregiver's well-being.[3] Some of the resources that Lois had available to her were her sister and her brother-in-law who also lived in the home and were very supportive to her. She also had other siblings who visited. Additionally, her RN degree was a valuable resource in that it helped her in knowing how to provide care to her bedridden mother and care for a serious pressure sore.

Lois explained, "The thing I miss the most about taking care of her is that I don't have a doctor to tell me *what* to do. Then we come up with all these questions: Should we do this? Should we do that? It's my responsibility, and I certainly have the time. I don't have any children or grandchildren; and if I wasn't caring for her, I'd probably be doing something for somebody else. When she quits eating or drinking for a long time, this bothers me because I'm responsible for her care. I should do something. I'm in a schizophrenic position. I'm her daughter and I'm her nurse, and I think I put the nursing part first."

Lois continued, "The thing that I've done for the last several years is fight a pressure sore on her hip. It breaks through. We finally got it healed up; when we do, it looks nice. I feel real happy about that, 'cause I know what it means to have a pressure sore to take care of. I feel like it's my responsibility. I feel glad I can do it. She took care of me for eighteen years."

Fulfilling the call to become a caregiver can provide a source of valuable personal satisfaction. Families may be drawn closer together through the expression of care, love, and concern for an aging parent by the fulfillment of family obligations and the call to fulfill a duty. Some caregivers believe their assistance enhances their parent's well-being, which in turn enhances the caregiver's feelings of mastery.[4] For Lois, providing care to her mother was no doubt a sacrifice, but one that she found to be rewarding because she saw it as something a daughter does for her mother. It didn't mean, however, that she did not experience some emotional strain or frustration at times.

"You just have to be on duty," she said. "And whenever the little bell rings, you just have to be there, or it'll ring more violently. Somebody's in there with her practically all the time. She demands or expects constant attention, really. I can't go to church. I can't go to the meetings, the clubs and things. It's just a different way of life, really. Just that you are a caretaker about twenty-four hours a day, and that certainly restricts the other things that you do."

Lois went on, "After a day and night or two of her hallucinations and her climbing, when there doesn't seem to be anything you can do for her or to calm her down, I think it's as much physical as it is emotional—just because you're tired of the whole ordeal."

A sense of satisfaction from providing care can be compromised when the older parent's physical and mental status deteriorates as it did with Lois's mother, Clara. She had some good days, but Lois described some very difficult days and nights, with no break. Other studies have described similar situations where the older parent requires a high level of personal care but is not mentally able to reciprocate in an emotional relationship. The caregiver is no longer allowed a break from her responsibilities, and it is then difficult for the caregiver to feel any sense of reward from providing care.[5]

Lois described things they used to be able to do more of when Clara was more cognitively capable and responsive. These things brought both of them pleasure.

"She enjoys the most looking at family pictures, pictures of way back when, and the children, great-grandchildren, the new babies in the family. There used to be a lot of things we did together, but now we don't."

Clara

Clara, Lois's mother, at 104 years of age had very low physical and cognitive functioning. Her cognitive functioning difficulties made the interview a bit difficult, but her daughter said that Clara was having a particularly good day and that hopefully I could get her to be responsive. Lois indicated that Clara cannot remember recent events or her home address, or find her way around the house (primarily because she is bedfast most of the time). At times, she had difficulty remembering words, instructions, or the day of the week. Her medical conditions included urinary problems, arthritis, and skin problems. I was surprised that she did appear to understand the questions I was asking of her. Her responses were brief, but coherent. She was pleasant, and she seemed to enjoy being asked questions. Her main concern was her lack of independence.

Clara said, "Not as much freedom. It bothers me to rely on help. I don't know, it's just the nature of me; independent, I guess."

She also provided brief responses about some positive things that she enjoys. She indicated that she felt close to her family at "supper time" and "bedtime" and that she appreciates that they "make her bed and make her good food."

Lois and Clara: Ten Years Later

You may recall that Lois, the daughter, at the time of the initial interview was eighty-one years old. At the time of the follow-up, she was now ninety-one and was living in her own home. At the time of the caregiving, even though she was the primary caregiver, she had her own home; however, she was often living with her sister and brother-in-law, where her mother was living, and she could provide round-the-clock care. Lois preferred not to be interviewed for the follow-up; however, her sister was more than willing, since ten years prior she had been part of the initial interviews. Her name was Betty, and she would not give her age; however, she was a few years younger than Lois. The interview with Betty follows:

Jeanne: *How long after the interview ten years ago did you continue caring for your mother, here in your home?*

Betty: She was just here one more year. She still had a sharp wit.

Jeanne: *Why did you decide to stop caring for her here?*

Betty: Well, she lost weight, and she got bedsores. Finally, the tissues just broke down and they were so very painful. And so finally she just decided she had had enough. She also got chills. She refused to eat, and I don't know if it was she didn't want to live or if it was the pain. That was the last couple of months.

Jeanne: *How was the decision made not to put your mother in a nursing home? How did you decide?*

Betty: Well, my sister, Lois, was just a natural-born nurse; she just took care of everyone. Mother was in the nursing home for a short time when she had broken her arm. She didn't like it, and we didn't like it.

Jeanne: *Did the quality of your relationship change in any way as your mother's health began to further deteriorate? If so, in what way?*

Betty: I don't know that there was. Nobody likes being cared for like that, but she accepted it as a fact of life. And I know she appreciated it.

Jeanne: *In what way did the household functioning change as the result of the change in your mother's health and residence?*

Betty: My sister, Lois, lived here for a while after that; not too long. She lives alone. I was the administrator, so that made me very involved doing the necessary things. We always had two people here. So I could go to the grocery store if I needed to.

Jeanne: *After the death of your mother, how did you feel?*

Betty: It is an adjustment, but you know it's coming. It has to, and you never are willing to give up your mother, but when it gets to that stage where she is suffering, then you have to be thankful for the relief. She had become a lot quieter through the years. Less responsive.

Jeanne: *Did it worry you that she was going to pass away soon, and knowing it would be here and you would see it, did that bother you?*

Betty: No, it isn't pleasant, but we are a very practical family. She was ready to go; she wasn't fighting it.

Jeanne: *Did you feel that old conflicts were resolved? Did new conflicts arise? If so, in what way?*

Betty: Not really, no; she was very cooperative. Our family is not a conflict family; it's just not our style. We also lived at a distance when we were younger so there wasn't too much meddling. She never interfered with our lives.

Jeanne: *Was accepting the death of your mother more difficult because of the relationship you shared?*

Betty: No, I don't think so. Having a secure home of my own was the key in that. It helped me. If you were in an unhappy situation, that would increase the loss. Dying is part of nature's process.

Jeanne: *Was there a sense of loss, or was there a sense of relief after your mother's death? If so, in what way?*

Betty: It was horrible, as her skin got worse, so it was a relief for her. The nurse that came to see her had a cure for the bedsores. And she could do it. They packed it with seaweed, and it healed.

Jeanne: *In what way did the household functioning change as the result of your mother's absence?*

Betty: I think the hardest thing was that she had been in our bed, and I think the hardest thing was getting back in the bed. We moved back in there.

Jeanne: *Looking back to ten years ago and thinking about now, has your perception of the caregiving situation changed in any way? If so, in what way?*

Betty: No, I have no regrets. Good memories, and everything. She wasn't really demanding. She suffered, and when she needed things she asked for them. When she needed attention she asked for it.

Jeanne: *Looking back to ten years ago and thinking about now, has your perception of your relationship with your mother changed in any way? If so, in what way?*

Betty: Well, like anything, you would improve if you had another chance. If I knew then what I know now, it would have been a little different.

Jeanne: *Like what types of things are you thinking about?*

Betty: Spend more time with her. Those kinds of things. Well, now I am always thinking about our family history. I want to know how everyone fit into the family tree. And now, I will never know because my mother was the only one who knew. Our family—our extended family—was never close. We never had cousins to play with. We had them scattered around, but they never came around when I was old enough to remember.

Jeanne: *Is there anything else you would like to add or that you think would be important for me to know?*

Betty: No, I think she was satisfied with her life and her lifestyle. She had a very practical family that supported her. She had an appreciation for nature; this is the way life is. She found where she is at, like plants grow and die. You have to look at God's point in life.

DISCUSSION OF INITIAL INTERVIEWS

In the case of Janice and her mother, Amelia, there were supports used within the household and some support from outside the house with a mental health professional. Amelia functioned fairly well physically, but she had some cognitive issues in terms of mood swings and depression, which as we heard from the interviews was very hard on the family. Lois had support within the household as well. Clara was bedridden and had poor cognitive functioning. Both daughters had been caring for their mothers for one year. However, Janice's responses to the interview questions indicated that she was experiencing more burden and emotional strain than Lois. From the interviews, it appeared that Lois was better able to accept her situation and her restrictions. Perhaps, because of her mother's advanced age, the kinds of changes she was dealing with in her mother seemed easier to accept, and the fact that she had been a nurse gave her the skill level to handle the care that was required. Lois had a strong sense of duty and family obligation. She also had a good relationship with her mother and with her sister who lived in the home and those sisters who lived outside the home.

Janice felt disillusioned about the reality of growing old and caring for her mother. I think that perhaps because of her mother's relative youth (seventy-eight years old) that it made it harder to accept the decline she was witnessing, particularly in her mother's behavior. After her mother moved in, a whole history of emotions was brought to the surface. In addition to having to deal with her mother's behavior problems and mood swings, she was reminded of her mother's selfish and controlling ways. Both she and her mother were unhappy with the situation. Also, the caregiver's spouse and fifteen-year-old daughter did not get along with the care-receiver, adding further tension to the shared-residence situation. Janice's spouse told me, "I have a controversy with my family. They feel I need to hush hush around her, not to say anything which will upset her. I think this is ridiculous; nobody dares to say something, and I do. I don't think she should be allowed to sit and say whatever she wants to say or do nothing, without any reactions. She is a very immature person." In fact, this was a real issue with the twenty-year-old son and the eighteen-year-old son, who both felt their father should be kinder and more understanding of their grandmother.

Janice's sons appeared to have an understanding of the situation far beyond their years. However, Janice shared a history of some conflict, growing up, that her sons had not experienced. When Janice's eighteen-year-old son asked her why his grandmother did not show her appreciation the way she showed him appreciation, Janice replied, "That is because old habits are hard to break."

Lois appeared to view her situation as just being part of her life, whereas Janice seemed to view her situation as disruptive and unordinary. She did say that she imagined her parents still living and living with her, but she had not imagined the current situation she now found herself in.

If the discussion of the two mother/daughter pairs were limited to the health condition of the mothers and the amount of care and assistance needed from their daughters, then Lois would immediately be perceived as having a much greater burden then did Janice. However, the interviews brought out more significant factors than the simple fact that, with only family supports, Lois had to care for a bedridden, cognitively impaired mother, while Janice had support from her sons and outside professional support in caring for her mother, with much less demanding physical and cognitive problems to deal with. However, Janice's mother, Amelia, experienced bouts of depression (as diagnosed by a mental health professional) and mood swings; she would go from extremely talkative to being hostile and agitated. At one time, before the intervention of medication, she indicated to one of her grandsons that she wanted to commit suicide. These changes were upsetting to the individual members of the family as well as the overall household functioning.

Unfortunately, Janice had her own set of challenges—her rejection of her changing situation and responsibilities, her resentment of her mother's past and present behavior and attitudes, and the lack of cohesion and cooperation within her own family. This was, no doubt, adding to the strain that Janice was feeling as she was certainly doing her best to navigate a very complex situation. She was trying her hardest to still raise her family, to be a good wife, to work part-time, to be a good daughter, and to manage her mother's care. She was being pulled in so many directions, and she was trying to keep everyone in the household happy. Her husband and fifteen-year-old daughter were very unhappy, and her two sons were making the most of a difficult situation.

Lois's view of her situation and her acceptance of and sense of security with her place and purpose in life—coupled with a good mother/ daughter relationship and the help and understanding of other family members—left her less concerned with what was happening to her and more satisfied with what was being achieved in this phase of her life. The difference in the sense of burden in the two cases was more about variations in attitudes, family dynamics, and interpersonal relationships than because of actual differences in needs and resources. Janice's mother, Amelia, had severe mood swings, powerful feelings of resentment, and a tendency to withdraw from the world around her. Essentially the same instability, resentment, rejection, and withdrawal were dominant factors in the behavior of three of the five people who might have been contributing to her care. Only the two sons of the family showed consistency of attitude, compassion, will, and a strong sense of family.

Conversely, Lois and her family supports, while realistic about their own feelings, were consistently responsible, positive, giving, and cooperative. Sympathetic to Clara's feelings and needs, they willingly made sacrifices for her, and they knew that she recognized and appreciated what they did for her. She was seen not as an undeserved, unavoidable, unwelcome burden but, instead, as a respected family member who had done her share for many years and now needed and deserved their help. It seems quite clear that the degree of burden felt by the people involved in the two families derived more from a projection of their own feelings and values than from the physical bases of their responsibilities.

The mothers, Amelia and Clara, were not affectionate, did not contribute to the household or assist their daughters, rarely participated in any activities with their daughters or other family members, did not perceive loneliness as a significant problem, and would have preferred more privacy. Amelia periodically set the table or fed the dog, but assistance was not on a regular basis. The chief difference between the mothers was their relationship with their daughters. Amelia had a history of a poor relationship with her daughter as well as her son-in-law, and she was very much centered on her own needs. Clara had a strong sense of family and had always had a good relationship with her daughter. Even though Clara had the lowest physical and cognitive functioning, she was very much considered a part of the family, rather than someone to be managed or tolerated. The main satisfactions for the mothers, Amelia and Clara, were moments when they felt close to their daughters.

Chapter Three

Personal Perfection versus Personal Connection

The two households in this comparison were slightly different in that one pair was a mother/daughter and the other pair was a niece caring for her aunt. Sadly, in this particular case, the daughter of the aunt had "kicked her out of the house" and said she did not have time to care for her, which is why the niece took her aunt to live with her. The niece shared with me that she felt like her aunt was "very much a part of the family" and that she felt like a daughter to her aunt. The comparison of these two households serves to highlight the differences in the perceptions of the caregiving arrangement that each caregiver had, even though the functioning level of their care-recipients was quite similar.

KATE AND MARGARET

Kate

Kate was forty-five years old, divorced, and employed full-time, and she had a seventeen-year-old daughter. She had not relied upon any form of support from either inside or outside the household during the nine years she had been caring for her eighty-five-year-old mother, Margaret. Kate's daughter was not helpful to either her mother or her grandmother. Kate told me that her daughter often entered into screaming matches with Margaret. Kate and her mother had very little interaction other than Kate helping her mother with bathing, dressing, and medications. They had almost no communication and displayed no affection. Kate said that she had not expected to become a caregiver. She explained to me that she is a perfectionist, and everything had to be just perfect. In fact, this was to the extreme, and Kate saw a mental health therapist on a regular basis for help in dealing with this issue. Finances were not a problem in this household, at least not for Kate. She did share with me Margaret's financial situation.

When I asked Kate if she had expected to become a caregiver, her response indicated that she had dreams that really did not mesh with the reality of her current life.

Kate answered, "I just always dreamed of some glamorous career where I could not be here, not be in this town, be somewhere else. In reality, I probably would have been here anyway. But I mean my dream was to be someplace else. I'd like to think I'd be out in Colorado or New Mexico, just as much as I say I'd never get married again. To be with someone, a companion. Just having an easier life. And life isn't all that rough. I mean it's stressful, but it's not impossible. It's just that some days it would be nice to not have a care in the world, you know."

During my interview with Kate, a surprising element emerged. It appeared that Kate cherished the role of caregiver more than she cherished the relationship with her mother. She had a complete and total personal commitment to the role of caregiving, as if it were a job. The care she provided seemed to make her feel more worthy, needed, and appreciated, and it gave her a great sense of accomplishment. She had very little communication with her mother and no shared activities, and they spent very little time together, other than watching some TV together.

The following quotes highlight that she is a perfectionist and that she must, as she says, "do it all—and do it all *right*." Kate talked about seeing a therapist for being so demanding of herself. She put a tremendous amount of pressure on herself. Many years later, when Kate was no longer providing care to her mother, one would think that she would feel more freedom to pursue the kinds of things that maybe she had always dreamed of doing, but this was not the case. She ended up seeking out others to care for, whether it was a neighbor or someone from her church.

"It's my job," Kate said. "I don't resent it. It's what I feel I should do. I guess it's my responsibility because she raised me. It's pay-back time. It's not like, well, you did it for me, so I have to do it for you. It's just this is what parents and children do for each other. That's really the way I feel about it. I have to live with myself, and I couldn't if I just shipped her off to a nursing home. I can honestly say I give 110 percent, maybe not with the best attitude. But I do the job. I do what has to be done."

This was Kate's response when asked about any support she might have. You will see that the first three sentences are identical to her earlier response: "It's my job. I don't resent her for it. It's what I feel I should do. I have to be the best caregiver. I have to be the best, you know. I've got to do it right. Like I told you before, I see a mental health therapist. We work on this. I'm very intolerant of people who don't demand the best of themselves. I don't demand the best of other people, but I demand the best of myself. I feel I should be able to do it all—and do it all right. If Joe Blow can't do it, that's not my problem. But I should be able to, and there's no excuse why I shouldn't. I'm much harder on myself than anybody else would be."

In Kate's response about her mother's functioning level, you see her worry about what might happen and what decisions she will have to make. You also you see her commitment or almost compulsiveness to having to do what is "right." She said, "I know it's not gonna get any better. It's just like waiting for the other shoe to drop. I mean every day when I get up in the morning it's like—well, is she gonna be alive? What decisions am I gonna have to make? Just the worry of what to do. I want to do what's right. You know it has to be right, when you're in this mode of it has to be right."

I asked Kate how she felt about having to perform various caregiving tasks. Not surprisingly, Kate's emotional strain showed through in several of her responses: "Just sometimes [I feel frustrated] when she can't do anything for herself. It doesn't make me mad. It's just like I'm so tired. It's just like—why can't you just do something? But it doesn't make me mad. I understand, but yet I'm still so tired. Oh yeah, frequently I feel emotionally drained, totally wiped out. My daughter and my brother are not helpful, at all. When my brother visits, once a year, he tries to do some things around the house."

Kate continued, "I have to come home at noon to fix her lunch and make sure she eats, and make sure she goes to the bathroom, and I have to come right home after work. I don't have the option of going out with the girls for a drink, or you know, runnin' shopping or doin' anything. I have to come right home. The stress is there of not knowing what I'm gonna find when I walk in at noon [afraid she'll be dead]. No. I pretty much do what I wanna do. After I get her to bed, if I wanna go out I can. I know this is my job for now, and it's not gonna go on forever."

When I asked Kate about spending time with her mother and feelings of affection, these were her responses: "We can't. I mean we sit and watch TV together. But she can't do anything anymore. We don't sit there and talk because she has trouble hearing. I mean we don't have a lot to talk about. But I'm just more comfortable out in the kitchen, so I just usually stay there most of the time. We really don't spend a lot of time together."

She added, "No. I don't feel affectionate. I don't feel close. It's always been that way. I don't feel. I'm not a very affectionate person because I don't feel affectionate towards anybody. I don't hug my daughter. I don't hug my mother."

Kate felt good about the caregiving situation, but not because she felt good about her mother or about their relationship. It was more about how the caregiving situation made Kate feel, in terms of her own self-worth. Later, in the ten-year follow-up interview with Kate, you will see that this sentiment did not change.

Margaret

Kate's mother, Margaret, was eighty-five years old and had no problems with cognitive functioning; however, she did have a little trouble with memory. She was a little bit difficult to interview because she was not as verbal in her responses and seemed to be more interested in watching TV. Her health conditions included heart problems and diabetes. Her responses to the interview questions were a testimonial to the gratitude that she felt for being cared for by her daughter.

"Life's much easier," Margaret said. "She does everything. I am so thankful to have them [daughter and granddaughter]. Well, I'd be pretty dumb if I didn't appreciate it. I don't do anything for 'em. Oh, I listen. But not being out and around, I'm not about to give advice. They're the ones that do the doing. They take such good care of me that I don't have to ask for stuff."

Kate and Margaret: Ten Years Later

Kate was very willing to be interviewed and seemed to be happy about the opportunity to talk, once again, about her situation in life. Kate's mother had died, but before she died, she was living in a nursing home.

Jeanne: *Why did you decide to stop caring for your mother here, in your home?*

Kate: She had fallen, and the doctor at the hospital said she could not come home; it was time for her to go to the nursing home.

Jeanne: *Did the quality of your relationship change in any way as your mother's health began to further deteriorate? If so, in what way?*

Kate: We never really had a relationship when I was young. So it was not much different. Well, she became more dependent. She knew she couldn't do it herself—that she had to depend on me.

Jeanne: *It wasn't like you became closer?*

Kate: Well, no, but um . . . I would get her up in the morning, get her dressed, go to work, and at noon, I would come home and feed her, then go back to work. Then I would come home and stay home in the evening. But then it would get worse. It worried my daughter coming home from school and finding her.

Jeanne: *Was your mother helpful in making the decision to go to the nursing home? If so, in what way?*

Kate: I don't think she really understood at that point where she was. The whole time she was in the nursing home, I don't think she said ten words, and she just refused to eat, and she starved to death. She didn't want to be in the nursing home, and she wanted to die. She was eighty-seven.

Jeanne: *In what way did the household functioning change as the result of the change in your mother's health and residence?*

Kate: It felt empty; the house just felt empty. I had the dog and I had the cats, but I would still get up in the morning and still want to get up and go in and get her ready. Because by then it was such a routine. So then I started at noon, and I would go over to the nursing home. And then again at the end of the day, so now that was my routine, so I was there twice a day. It was empty in the morning. I had it down to a science. And that is how I stayed thin at the time; I was so focused. After she died, I was really lost. I had no one to take care of. She had been my whole world for so long. Well, I ended up at the doctor's office with serious depression. And to be perfectly honest, I still have to take antidepressants. If I do without them for more than three days I just sit and bawl. I just start crying for no reason.

Jeanne: *Do you mean that she was your whole world, like the relationship, or the care you provided, the routine?*

Kate: Yes, the care provider. And to be honest, there was . . . I felt like I was really accomplishing something because I could get it all done. I could do the work at the office and take care of her. And because I had such a schedule I was focused. And I lost that focus. I knew I couldn't fall apart because I had to take care of her.

Jeanne: *It wasn't the relationship—it was the focus and the care providing?*

Kate: I found someone to take care of. The lady that works at our church—we would go out for lunch, and as her health started to fail, she depended on me more. I was the one who had to put her in the hospital, because she kept falling, and then in the nursing home. She had kids; she wouldn't even let them in the house when she was in the nursing home. I was the only one with a key. I took care of her for a year and a half. She just passed away this last November. So now I am back at the same place, what do I do? I would go visit her at the nursing home. It gave me satisfaction. We were with her all day. She had a stroke, and I wanted to be there—because no one should die alone.

Jeanne: *Do you feel old conflicts with your mother were resolved? Did new conflicts arise?*

Kate: No, there were no new conflicts. My father taught me early in life [that] there are three ways of doing things in life: [he said,] "the right way, the wrong way, and your mother's way. And you might as well do it your mother's way, 'cause you might as well be happy." I grew up knowing that, and we did things her way.

Jeanne: *So you never got into any conflicts with her—you just did your thing and went about the care?*

Kate: No, I just did my thing, didn't fight with her on anything.

Jeanne: *Was there a sense of loss, or was there a sense of relief after your mother's death? If so, in what way?*

Kate: It was a loss; it still isn't a relief. I still feel the sense of loss. If I had it my way, I would still be taking care of her. I don't know why that is.

Jeanne: *Is it that you miss your mother or—what is it? What do you miss?*

Kate: The caregiving, somebody that really needs me. No, that is a very selfish thing to say. And I am one of the caregiving deacons at church.

Jeanne: *What about it provided you with satisfaction?*

Kate: I guess that she just simply depended on me for food and everything to be done. I brought clothes to be washed because she didn't want them washed at the nursing home [now talking about the neighbor she cared for]. And her kids told me she didn't leave anything in her will to me, and they asked how much do I want for caring for her. And I said I don't want anything; I took care of her because I loved her.

Jeanne: *Looking back to ten years ago and thinking about now, has your perception of the caregiving situation changed in any way? If so, in what way?*

Kate: No, I felt that I did the best job I could at the time, and I still feel I did. I don't have any regrets. Like I should have stayed home with her? I mean, God was looking out for her.

Jeanne: *You said that you gave 110 percent.*

Kate: Yes, and therefore I really don't have any regrets.

Jeanne: *Looking back to ten years ago and thinking about now, has your perception of your relationship with your mother changed in any way? If so, in what way?*

Kate: No, it wasn't kissy, huggy. It was what it was.

Jeanne: *Is there anything else you would like to add or that you think would be important for me to know?*

Kate: No, I just hope you do another follow-up in ten years [laughs]!

TAMMY AND DOROTHY

Tammy

Tammy, thirty-five years old, was a niece caring for her seventy-four-year-old aunt. Tammy was married, had a fifteen-year-old daughter, and worked full-time. She had a private duty nurse who came twice a day to assist with care of her aunt Dorothy, which she found to be very helpful. Her husband and daughter had a good relationship with

Dorothy and tried to help out by doing little things for her, such as propping up pillows or making something for her to eat. There was a high level of communication and feelings of closeness between Tammy and Dorothy. Tammy had not expected to become a caregiver, but she said that she considered her aunt very much a part of the family and that she felt like a daughter to her aunt. They both shared with me that Dorothy's daughter had "kicked her out of the house" and said that she did not have time to care for her. Finances were not a problem in this household.

In the case of Tammy providing care, we hear from her quotes that caregiving was not a disruption in her life and that she felt it was simply a family obligation to care for her aunt, since her aunt's immediate family no longer wanted to provide care. She also mentioned that she loved her, which is more than feeling obligated.

Tammy said in her interview, "Life is really not that different than what I expected. I expected it to change somewhat, and it's changed in the direction I knew it would. But it wasn't a problem. I felt that was what I should do. It was my Christian duty to do that—and then the love that I have for her. Giving her love is easy. I mean it's just something that would be the easiest."

"We enjoy having her here," Tammy continued. "It's not a burden. It makes me feel good. We're all selfish creatures to some extent, and it makes me feel good about myself. It would have been very hard for me to live with myself if I hadn't. I guess it was a decision between God and me to decide if it was right for us. That it was right to do it. We don't walk around on tiptoes with her, and she doesn't either. If she's cold, she'll tell you she's cold. We don't treat her like a guest. I mean she's part of the family. There are times it isn't all perfect. I wouldn't be honest if I said everything's just roses, because she can be very contrary sometimes."

Tammy had support that she found to be very helpful. She had a private duty nurse for a short period in the morning and then in the evening, and she also had family support, which she described as being her sister, her mother, her husband, and her daughter. Studies on caregiving and support have found that it isn't really about how much or the type of support that was important, it was more about what the caregiver perceived as helpful.[1] Support can, no doubt, help in alleviating the burden felt by caregivers; however, it may not necessarily increase satisfaction with the situation by improving the quality of the relationship. For example, some caregivers may have more time to themselves if their parent is in adult day care for several hours a day, but then they may feel irritated that their spouse isn't providing assistance or emotional support. Outside support also does help improve communication between mothers and daughters or alleviate long-standing conflict.

Tammy described the caregiving support she had: "My sister, my mother, which is her sister, basically those are the only two. Oh sure, my husband does things. My daughter does things. I don't want my daughter to do things. I don't want to burden my husband or my daughter. But my daughter does things without me asking. She'll watch TV with her; she'll fix her lunch sometimes. My husband will fix her dinner if I'm working late—or prop her pillows up. Just little personal things like that. He'll get things for her and go and check on her, and he folds and washes her clothes, too [laughs]. The private duty nurse is helpful. She comes for two hours in the morning and then one hour in the evening, between 6:00 p.m. and 7:00 p.m. This allows me to get my stuff done so I can visit with my aunt."

Tammy described feeling close to her aunt and also being affectionate with her: "It's just spontaneous, I think. You know, of course it's your emotions when you're sad, or when she particularly said something that makes you laugh, that's funny. Affection is something that just comes naturally. It's hard to describe. I feel close to her because I know she loves my daughter very much; therefore, we have that in common."

Dorothy

Dorothy was seventy-four years old and had very low physical functioning, but she did not appear to have any serious cognitive functioning issues. However, she did tend to ramble off track during the interview. Her health conditions included urinary problems, arthritis, emotional problems, and skin problems.

Dorothy's main concern was loneliness, and her greatest satisfaction was that she had her niece. She expressed how grateful she was to have her, since her own family did not want to care for her. I can't imagine how emotionally painful this must have been for Dorothy, to know that her own children did not want her.

Dorothy began, "Well, yeah, you know, I miss my husband, you know. He died in 1989. I am more lonely here. I had neighbors there that came over, and see, I don't know anybody here. See she works. But right now the little girl is here, but when school starts, she'll be gone to school. Then, see, I'll be all alone except for the dog."

She continued, "I'm close to my sister [the niece's mother], and I'm close with Tammy and her sisters. I just know I'm better off. I'm thankful to have somebody that would take me in. She's more like a daughter than she is like a niece. I have a daughter, and she didn't want me."

Note: Tammy had moved away, and I was unable to locate her for the ten-year follow-up interview.

DISCUSSION OF INITIAL INTERVIEWS

Even though Margaret's and Dorothy's physical functioning levels were almost identical, the caregivers' burden levels and ways of handling their burden were very different. Kate admitted to being a perfectionist who demanded the best of herself. Regardless of the amount of actual burden from caring for her mother, she put tremendous pressure on herself to do everything right. For her, "doing it right" was the focus of caregiving. She had very little communication with her mother and a low-quality relationship; there was little give-and-take, no participation in shared activities other than watching some TV, and no display of affection. Unlike Tammy, who had help from her husband and daughter, as well as a private duty nurse, Kate had no outside support and no assistance from her family. Tammy had an excellent relationship with her aunt, high communication, a strong sense of family, and shared affection. She also indicated that it was her "Christian duty" to provide care for her aunt. Her religious beliefs possibly assisted her in keeping a positive attitude. Tammy, unlike Kate, was not affected in terms of disrupted life course expectations, personal lifestyle, and role strain. Also, she had friends over frequently and, therefore, was not as isolated as Kate was. The primary elements resulting in the differences between Kate and Tammy were relationship quality and perceived level of support. Kate had a poor-quality relationship with her mother and had no support system. Tammy had a loving, close relationship with her aunt and had a supportive spouse and daughter coupled with the assistance of a private duty nurse.

In Kate's situation, reported burden reflects the impact of a collage of problems and frustrations with her mother as the focal point, rather than a statement of the degree of actual burden resulting from the caregiving process. Kate acknowledged no support: her daughter appeared to constitute added burden, rather than a source of support; Kate's husband was absent because of a divorce; and Kate's brother visited only rarely. Her isolation was possibly an outgrowth of her compulsive insistence upon perfection, her stated lack of feelings of affection for anyone, and her admitted strong feelings of intolerance toward people who did not demand the best of themselves. Her need for and stability to attain perfection left her exhausted and frustrated. She strongly felt that her life should somehow be more than it was: "I just always dreamed of some glamorous career where I could not be here, not be in this town." Still, she had no concrete idea as to what her life should be, where she should be, what she could do to improve her life. She seemed trapped in the conviction that her life really could not have been any different, anyway. Her insecurity and confusion were also reflected in frequent statements that were either partially or wholly self-contradictory or that contradicted other statements made during the interview. She feels no affection for her mother, yet she feels that she must be a perfect caregiver because she owes care and can accept nothing short of perfection from herself. Although Kate had no support system, what she did for her mother appeared far less burdensome than the problems, needs, and attitudes that she brought to the task. I feel tremendous empathy for Kate because she was aware of her need for perfection and talked about how "totally wiped out" she was, and yet she couldn't seem to break out of this pattern of care that she had become committed to or almost had trapped herself in because she was unable to break up the routine. When she finally did have freedom from no longer providing care to her mother, she took on the care of others in order to keep a "schedule" and to keep "focused" and so she "wouldn't fall apart." Kate needed the role of caregiving, and it was wonderful that it could fulfill her and allow her to give back to someone else who needed her care.

Tammy had an open, loving, and giving nature, which allowed her to accept her responsibilities and maintain good relationships with other family members who were willingly supportive of her. While it is obvious that the help she received lightened her burden, it's worthy to note that her attitudes, values, and personal conduct led others to want to help her, which further lightened her burden by enabling her to receive psychological benefit from family relationships and from the appreciation she received for what she did. Perhaps Tammy and Kate were not so different—they each received a sense of fulfillment in caring for family.

Both Margaret and Dorothy were happy with their living arrangement. However, Dorothy (the aunt) did mention that she misses her home. Privacy was not a problem, nor was dissatisfaction with care, for either care-receiver. Dorothy had some difficulty with loneliness and feeling that she was not able to give back to her niece or care for others the way she used to. She commented that she was "used to helping somebody else—not somebody helping me." However, these factors were not troublesome to Margaret. Satisfaction for both care-receivers stemmed from feeling appreciative of their caregivers and the tasks the caregivers performed. Both care-receivers felt a sense of family orientation, but only Dorothy mentioned that there was actual physical expression of affection between her and her niece. In addition, only Dorothy participated in and enjoyed activities with her caregiver, which included long talks about church and the Bible. Only between Tammy and Dorothy was there a high level communication and a high-quality relationship. The focus for Kate and Margaret appeared to be on performing routine tasks and activities.

Chapter Four

Emotional Interference versus Personal Fulfillment

The mother/daughter pairs in these two households were similar in that the care-receivers, a mother and a mother-in-law, had high physical and cognitive functioning; however, the daughters reported very different feelings about their caregiving situations. What was accounting for the differences in their perceived levels of burden and satisfaction?

KIM AND EMMA

Kim

Forty-four-year-old Kim had been caring for her sixty-six-year-old mother-in-law for four years; she was married and employed out of her home full-time. She used adult day care as a support but felt she had little if any support from her family. Kim indicated that her husband was not helpful with caregiving tasks, and her ten- and fourteen-year-old daughters occasionally did what they could to help out around the house. She had a very poor relationship with her mother-in-law, Emma. Kim did indicate that she had expected, at some point, to become a care-giver for one of her own or her husband's parents. She also suggested that finances were a problem for the household.

Kim described starting out feeling like she wanted to provide care to feeling constrained: "I don't know what I expected or didn't expect. But it went from, I want to do everything for her to, now I almost wish she weren't here, sometimes. If I wanted to go to, I mean, I'd be free to come and go as I please. If I wanted to say or do something, I wouldn't have to think about saying or doing it twice. I think I'd be one, so relaxed, not so always on edge, probably go away more. Just, I guess I'm a free spirit, so I guess just more free spirited, I guess. But now it's always this thing you gotta remember about, when I'm away from the house."

I asked Kim about the impact of having to perform caregiving tasks, and she said that it was not the tasks that bothered her. She went on to describe what did bother her.

"I'm not affected," she said. "It doesn't bother me really. It's so many other things that have nothing to do with this kind of stuff [caregiving tasks] that I find irritating. Eating with her mouth open. She'll come in from day care with these little nursery rhymes. She's so excited. I can't stand them anymore. I don't want to hear her nursery rhymes. I don't want to know about her nursery rhymes. She'll come home with these little drawings that she did. I mean we get so tired of this. But to her it's everything, and logically you know that. But it's enough!"

Kim continued, "Sometimes I get really upset with Emma, and my husband's attitude about it is, 'She doesn't ask for much, so why?' I say, ''Cause it's annoying me. Speak to her.' And it's like, but he's not here and he doesn't have to deal with it, and he doesn't deal with it. It's constant between him and her. Guys, I know what I'm doing. It's constantly a battle over her. I'm the one in charge. I hate to use that word. I feel sometimes he has to stick up for me and he won't, and he doesn't, and if I say anything, he says I'm picking on his mother. But I'm not. I'm just trying to organize. I was told that his mother is his business, and yet he does nothing. I can't talk to my husband. If I go to talk to him, he gets mad and says I'm picking on her, even if I haven't talked to her. He doesn't want his mother talked about at all. If there is anything that's a problem if you ignore it, it doesn't exist. I think a lot of men are like that."

Kim clearly was more frustrated with her husband, and not feeling supported by him, than she was with providing care to Emma. She didn't necessarily want someone to help with any specific tasks, but she wanted to feel like her husband "had her back" and that he supported her decisions, felt that she was making good decisions, and thought she was doing a good job. Kim needed validation for what she was doing.

Many of her statements appear startlingly harsh, but perhaps it is really more about the frustration she was feeling toward her husband and the strained relationship with him, rather than with Emma. Kim, at times, felt some empathy toward Emma for how her family treated her, but then she would become overwrought with her own emotional strain.

Kim had this to say in describing her frustrations with her mother-in-law, and she mentions the support of day care. Again, day care was important to Kim since she did not have the support of her husband.

"I just want to be free and not think," she said. "It's an emotional interference. It's frustration, you just get so tired of 'over and over and over.' I felt good when I got her into day care. I would have killed her had she not gone. It's hard with her because it's nothing that's really major. It's all the really fine things that bother you. I don't feel a close-ness to her. I don't feel that bonding, at all."

Kim talked about truly having felt sorry for Emma because of how Emma's immediate family treated her, but then she describes how her feelings changed: "I feel very bad for her that she's never had a decent life—that kind of thing. Before, I always felt sorry for her, I felt sorry for her, the way she was treated by her family. I have always felt sorry for her, 'cause they treat her like absolute garbage. Feeling sorry for her—that's changed. There are lots of days I've had enough, and I wish she weren't here. It's kind of an annoyance."

Besides support, another source of conflict between Kim and Emma was their different religious beliefs. During the interview, Kim said, "She's only for her church." Emma said, during the interview, "She'll [Kim] say, anybody that don't share our beliefs can get out."

These comments, and some of the statements you will read in a moment, made by Emma, clearly show there was a lack in the household for respect of differences, a respect for boundaries, and a respect for supporting relationships. Many of the essential skills that could have been helpful in this caregiving situation boil down to the things that we find in good communication. Perhaps Kim, her husband, and Emma could have had a more positive outcome if they had practiced empathy, respect, and open-mindedness.

It is also important to note that finances were of concern in this household to both the caregiver and to the care-receiver. Along with household tasks and social/emotional tasks, financial tasks often are a part of providing care to one's aging parents. These might include

writing checks, paying bills, proving financial support, helping manage
resources, and paying for essentials.[1] Inadequate financial resources
can cause additional stress for the caregiver who may also be managing the household budget.[2] During the interview, Kim did not dwell on
financial problems but did indicate this was a problem when completing
a questionnaire on household resources. Finances were also mentioned
in the ten-year follow-up interview. This may have been a contributing
factor to some of the resentment that Kim was feeling toward Emma.

Emma

Kim's mother-in-law, Emma, was sixty-six years old and had insuf-
ficient income to meet her needs. She had relatively high physical
functioning and no problems with cognitive functioning. She did have a
diagnosis of Parkinson's; however, it was early enough at this point that
she was not having issues with her activities of daily living.

During the interview with Emma, the main concerns that came to
light were issues of respect, privacy, and religious differences. She also
described helping with household tasks.

She said, "Well, you're just not your own boss. They just kind of ignore me. She [Kim] makes mountains out of molehills. Very few would
want to live that way."

"Everything has to be her way," Emma continued. "She watches everything I do. She won't leave me with the children by myself."

She also said, "We're not close. She don't make me feel that way.
She's against my religious beliefs. She doesn't have my same beliefs."

Emma described having to assist with household tasks: "I do mountains of laundry. I dry the dishes and put them away. But you get hollered at stuff you don't even do. She hollers loud at me. She'll say,
'Well, I believe my daughter.'" If something goes wrong in the household or something gets broken or misplaced, Emma said the caregiver
blames her when it may have been another family member's fault.

Few studies on caregiving have closely examined the specific prob-
lematic elements and/or issues associated with being a care-receiver,
particularly in a shared residence. This may be because it is difficult
to locate mother/daughter pairs who are living together and to identify
mothers who are cognitively capable of responding to interview questions. As you have read thus far, it is important to understand the unique

feelings and experiences of dependent, older adult women being cared for by their daughters.

Kim and Emma: Ten Years Later

Kim cared for her mother-in-law for roughly another six months before she and her husband made the decision to put her in the nursing home where she had been attending day care. Perspectives ten years later brought about some interesting insights into Kim's feelings about her mother-in-law and their relationship.

Jeanne: *Why did you decide to stop caring for her here?*

Kim: I couldn't—she was having accidents, wetting accidents. She was so weak and she wasn't eating, and the kids were at an age where they could understand. It was really hard on them. They would ask, "Why isn't Grandma trying to get better?" [Her daughters were ten and fourteen at the time.] My husband couldn't handle it. So, he was the reason she went there. He would never say it. But the sad thing is, is that his brother and sister would never help, not a penny, a dime, or a nickel.

Jeanne: *How was the decision made to have your mother cared for elsewhere? How did you decide where?*

Kim: It would be best, we thought. She had already been going there for day care. So it wasn't a big change, and we thought it was best to not put her anywhere else.

Jeanne: *Did the quality of your relationship change in any way as her health began to deteriorate? If so, in what way?*

Kim: I think part of the problem, and it's just my personality from working with the handicapped. And when I work with the handicapped people, I always expected them to take ten steps, and they would take three or four or five and it would be like "Wow." But if it hurt her at all she wouldn't even try. And that was the hardest thing. And for her to get better or at least maintain, she had to try; she was giving up. I never go to visit her. I will on her birthday and Christmas. But I will always say to my husband, "I made your mom a card," and I always make sure it is a religious card, 'cause I know she is religious. I always save the cards that you get in the mail. The ones with the Red Cross. I know she likes that, and he takes her cakes that I make her. She likes them. I take her things that she likes, but I don't interact with her. [It's interesting that we see a nice gesture of Kim being respectful about her mother-in-law's religion, by making her cards.]

Jeanne: *Did the quality of the relationship you shared with her help or hinder your decision to no longer provide care here?*

Kim: I think my bad attitude. I was the one who looked into the programs, and I just couldn't take it. So, I just said, "Fine, you take care of it. If I do such a bad job, then I will stop doing what I'm doing." I was the one getting social workers, and I am the one working on this. I'm the one who told you to bring her here. I don't know how to word it.

Jeanne: *Sounds as if you helped get the arrangements, but there were several things that added to her going to the nursing home—her health, the relationship, and you not feeling as if you had support. Was your mother-in-law helpful in making the decision? If so, in what way?*

Kim: Yeah, in a way she wanted to take the burden off of us. I don't know that for sure, but knowing her personality, she never wanted to be a problem, although she really did enjoy the food when she did eat. She never believed what the doctor would say. She would say it was due to her eyes if her stomach hurt. She had weird ideas. Parkinson's—she would pull out her false teeth, it was a whole other world I wasn't used to. She wouldn't exercise. It appeared to me she was very scared and afraid, and when she came here, she just seemed very different. She would never fight back. Dad wouldn't give in to her, so she came here with a few sheets and clothes; all her other belongings were left behind. [Up to this point, I thought she was widowed. This is where I learned she was still married. It appears there were some additional family issues and poor relationships. The fact that Kim did not know she was married also shows, again, some poor communication in the family.]

Jeanne: *How did your mother-in-law make the transition to where she is being cared for now?*

Kim: She loved it. Because everything was done for her, whereas here, I made her fight to do something, and there it was all done for her. If she was tired they let her sleep. She didn't want to bathe, so she didn't have to. And my husband gives her what she wants. And I would not take that away from her. All her life people just took, took, took, from her and never gave anything. She never had much. [Here we see some empathy from Kim toward Emma.]

Jeanne: *In what way did the household functioning change as the result of the change in your mother-in-law's health and residence?*

Kim: For one, I was less tired. My kids were in a lot of activities, plus her activities and stuff. And having to be here because she couldn't be left alone. You know, then I didn't have to make sure that she wasn't left alone. I had to make sure someone was in the house when I would leave. The meals would change. I think my husband and I did better. Because we didn't have to debate. And with your mother in the next room, "other" things don't occur. We kind of made a swing back together. And then the kids got their own room; I mean they were so crowded. But you know, when she came to us, I was about to paint all the rooms and I had her pick out her own paint and decorate her own room. So, it was her own room.

Jeanne: *After the final transition was made, how did you feel?*

Kim: Well, I didn't give up the relationship right away; it was a gradual stepping back. It was gradual; I would see her every Sunday and then every other Sunday, and then maybe once a month. But I would always bake her a birthday cake and bring it up there. I got her Christmas presents and all that. She likes soft candy because she can eat that. It can't take up space. One major difference is that she wears pants now. I don't know how they got her to do that. She would never wear pants. I felt relieved. I was really relieved; there was no more pressure.

Jeanne: *Did you realize how much pressure you were under?*

Kim: Right, you don't know until it's not there. I wanted to be the good daughter-in-law and the good wife. It was just very, very hard.

Jeanne: *Do you feel old conflicts were resolved? Did new conflicts arise? If so, in what way?*

Kim: I know she likes me. But I don't know, she never really talks. Not between her and me, it was between the children and her and between my husband and his sister; he does not talk to his sister at all.

There are certain things, like she wants to be cremated. Which is totally against my religion. She wants to have the service here. He [her husband] still says things like "You never really liked my mom." And I don't know what to say. I took care of her for four and a half years, and [he] never did anything. He never had to say that I did a great job or anything like that, but just to say that I never did anything, or didn't like her—just bull crap! I would do it all over again. [Kim still does not have the support or validation from her husband.]

Jeanne: *Why would you do it all over again?*

Kim: It's my husband; it's his mother.

Jeanne: *Looking back to ten years ago and thinking about now, has your perception of the caregiving situation changed in any way? If so, in what way?*

Kim: There is a part of me that is glad that it is over. I don't think it was bad; I look at it as it was difficult. And I would do it again in a minute, in a second. I have no regrets. I think I have taught my oldest daughter . . . she will always go there and visit. My younger daughter does not visit her and did not visit my mother in the hospital. She just can't take it. She is one who can work with children with mental disabilities but just can't do this. I still question, why did my mother-in-law let people use her like that? She was timid and afraid.

Jeanne: *Looking back to ten years ago and thinking about now, has your perception of your relationship with your mother-in-law changed in any way? If so, in what way?*

Kim: It is kind of a combination thing. I still feel sorry for her because I look at her life and I look at my life and I just don't see where she ever had a life. That has not changed. I am not angry with her; I am angry for her. I am angry that she never stuck up for herself.

Jeanne: *Is there anything else you would like to add or that you think would be important for me to know?*

Kim: I think it would be nice if more stuff were available nationwide for families going through it. There are day cares to help you, but there is nothing to help the family. Nothing in my house, so that she didn't have to leave, that could help me. Maybe someone to come in and relieve me. Someone to talk to. It is so weird because it was Kenny's mother, not mine, so we had it backwards. We need more support. She or he is under stress, just someone there. And I think at one point we went for counseling, I just couldn't do it anymore.

Jeanne: *I know you had said you didn't feel like you had the support from him that you needed.*

Kim: Just not even the physical things, but just the emotional support.

If Kim could have received the emotional support she wanted and needed from her husband, then the perception of the caregiving situation could have been much more positive. Here it is ten years later, and Kim still has tremendous empathy for Emma. She still tries to do nice things for her, and Emma's own family of origin (husband and kids, besides Kim's husband) has forgotten about her.

LUCILLE AND EDITH

Lucille

Sixty-five-year-old Lucille was employed part-time and widowed. She did not have help inside or outside of the home, and for three years, she had been caring for her eighty-six-year-old mother, Edith. She and her mother had an excellent relationship. Lucille was also caring for her eighty-nine-year-old aunt in the same household; her aunt was not physically impaired but had difficulty with cognitive functioning (she was not capable of being interviewed). The eighty-six-year-old mother and the eighty-nine-year-old aunt were sisters. Edith indicated to me that the two sisters spent quite of bit of time together. Edith, though fragile herself, felt responsible for her sister. Lucille explained that the two sisters often helped each other out. For example, Lucille's mother was capable of making sandwiches for the two of them as long as her sister, under her direction, brought her the necessary items to the table. It is remarkable that Lucille was navigating the care of both her mother and her aunt.

Lucille had not really expected to become a caregiver and definitely had other plans. I think what she has to say about how a family member becomes a caregiver is very insightful and may sound familiar to many caregivers. Research indicates that many caregivers who have raised their families now have to reconcile the demands of resuming care responsibilities with work.[3]

Lucille began, "I had reached a point where my family was raised and I was looking forward to a great deal of freedom. I would like to have had a trailer and trailered the U.S., but nothing's forever and right now this is fine. I fulfill a very important need, I have a lot of good supportive friends, and I try to keep a good attitude. Even as I went into it [caregiving], I wasn't sure that that's what I had become [a caregiver]. When it's your family, you're kind of eased into something, and then the next thing you know, bingo, there you are."

Lucille went onto say something that is very true about not doing all the things she would like to do, but then countered with important advice: "I can't do the things I want, to the degree that I would like to, absolutely not. This is priority to care for them. However, I'm good to myself in a lot of ways. I have a lot of nice interests."

Chapter 11 in this book talks about the importance of being good to yourself.

Lucille talked about how seeing her mother losing ground mentally was very difficult for her: "I find myself getting sharp with her, or short, because when I see something that I didn't used to see, it's upsetting to see. Oh boy! Here's an area where we're losing ground, or we're failing in. Emotionally, I think I don't want to see her slipping from me like this, so your natural reaction is, 'Why are you doing this? You didn't used to do this.' And it's out of love that this sharpness comes."

The following quote really summarizes Lucille's overall realistic attitude about caregiving and the general positive perception she has about her situation: "Caregiving has a lot of pluses, and very few negatives. I wouldn't have it any other way. It's the child in me that wants to run away. I just decided this is the way it is, and I feel good that I'm giving my mother good care. I'm doing what I should be doing at this point. There are days when it kind of wears me down, and I think that's the way it is right now. I just feel older. I feel stressed. I feel put upon, and I wouldn't be human if I didn't feel that way sometimes."

Lucille and Edith shared lots of activities together and have a quality relationship that includes good communication and affection. Lucille said, "I love to tease her. I love to play a joke on her. She loves that. I like to surprise her with pretty things. We like to go out to eat, and she enjoys that; so I make that something as nice as I possibly can. She's very nice to do things for because she always is so appreciative. I'd like to do more with her. She's limited on the things she can do. We play cards, share books, puzzles, and watch TV. We sit down before dinner and maybe have a glass of wine before dinner. I'll sit out on the porch with her. She'll come to my room a lot of times and sit on the bed and we'll talk for a while. We would probably spend more time together if my aunt wasn't living here."

Lucille continued, "She's limited on the things she can do. She's really good to bounce things off of, and I'll catch her up on the latest. It would be an impossible living situation if we didn't have the ability to give-and-take with each other. Our relationship is even better. It's never been a problem."

Lucille and her mother, Edith, were also affectionate with each other. Caregiving may be perceived as less stressful when the caregiver/ receiver relationship is characterized by strong bonds of affection.[4]

This is what Lucille had to say about the affection they shared: "Hugs and touches are important. There's always, 'Goodnight.' We never go to bed without saying 'Goodnight' to each other. Something that holds me back a little bit is I'm almost afraid to touch her sometimes. She's so fragile anymore. I just don't know hardly how to get a grip on her. The doctor said her bones are like powder."

Edith

Edith was eighty-six years old and had sufficient income to meet her needs. She had relatively high physical functioning and no problems with cognitive functioning. Her health conditions included high blood pressure and osteoarthritis, which did cause some frailty, but she was able to perform her activities of daily living. The main concerns for Edith were primarily her loss of independence and sometimes feeling lonely. Her satisfactions with the caregiving situation arose out of the quality relationship she shared with her daughter, which was characterized by good communication, affection, a sense of give-and-take, and shared activities.

Here are some of the things Edith had to say about loss of independence and loneliness: "Sometimes I think I'd like to have my own little apartment. But when you get older, that just doesn't happen. When you get older, you're dependent on somebody, whether it's family or strangers."

She continued, "Well, I think there is sometimes that you feel lonely. I really don't have much time to think about it. I do a lot of crossword puzzles. I read books a lot. So, I really don't let myself get—but I think lonely sometimes for the things we used to have. For the life we—but that's just memories. You get over it. It's just a passing."

Edith had this to say about the love they had for one another: "I'm always calling her honey. I tell her, 'Goodnight honey, I love you.' She's so good to us. We love each other. We don't always tell it. But on the whole, we do. I'm just glad we can be together."

Edith enjoyed and appreciated the nice things her daughter did for her, and she, in turn, tried to do things to be helpful and show her gratitude. Edith said, "She's always leaving little candy bars around in my chair and doing little surprises for me. Maybe she'll bring home a flower. She's always doing something. But whenever I can I do them. Just like I'll say let me peel potatoes. Anything I'm able to do."

Lucille and Edith enjoyed spending time together, whether it was engaging in an activity or just sitting together and reminiscing. Edith went on to say, "We play Skipbo [card game]. She and I enjoy that game. Then we sit around and visit and talk about old times together out in California. The good times we had."

"I am more than satisfied," Edith continued. "She just goes out of her way to make sure that we [she and her cognitively impaired sister] are happy, and she takes us out to eat, and she makes sure that we get out and takes us for drives. We went up to the Dinner Theatre. She makes sure we don't sit in the house all the time. She gets us out. Sometimes I feel like I'm keeping her from an active life. She needs to get away from old people."

Note: I was unable to locate Lucille for a ten-year follow-up interview. However, I did learn from someone who knew her that she had moved to a state that she had mentioned during our interviews. I assumed, given that her mother was eighty-six years old and her aunt was eighty-nine years old at the time of the initial interviews and it was now ten years later, that Lucille had moved away because both care-receivers were no longer living.

DISCUSSION OF INITIAL INTERVIEWS

The daughter-in-law, Kim, stated that she was constantly on edge and had found that putting up with her mother-in-law, Emma, kept her emotionally drained and frustrated half the time; in fact, she called caring for her an "emotional interference." Interestingly, however, she said that Emma's functioning level or the tasks involved in her care were not a problem, and she mentioned several times, during the interview, how sorry she felt for Emma. Her objections to Emma centered on such things as (from Kim's perspective) the messy bathroom, Emma eating with her mouth open, the tiresome nursery rhymes and the little drawings she bored them with when she came home from day care, the frustrating ways she bungled attempts at being helpful, the way she pushed her religion, and her refusal to do anything but "vegetate." However, Emma said that she did not mind depending on her family because she did enough for them to make up for her reliance on them, saying that she did mountains of laundry and helped with the housework. She also complained that they tended to ignore her, planning their things without her, and that the caregiver made mountains out of molehills, watched everything she did, would not trust her alone with the children. Emma said her caregiver often hollered at her in a loud voice, blamed her for things she was not responsible for, and believed the children's word over hers. She accused the caregiver of insulting her religion when talking to others in her presence.

Kim claimed that feeling sorry for Emma because her family treated her like garbage caused her to welcome her in the beginning, but their relationship had deteriorated so much that she no longer felt sorry for her and actually wished she were out of the house. She compared caring for her to washing dishes or doing laundry—"just something you do"—and said that they often went out without her because taking her was unpleasant. Kim so thoroughly resented the very presence of Emma that a question about emotional uplifts was answered with, "I felt good when I got her into day care. I would have killed her had she not gone." Undoubtedly, this is an overstatement, but it rings true as an indication of the relationship between Kim and Emma. She further complained that Emma was a constant point of contention between herself and her spouse. Kim said that he was defensive of his mother, refused to hear her be criticized, would not take Kim's side in conflicts with Emma, and yet refused to be of any help in taking care of his mother. Kim did credit her daughters with being of some occasional help, but she dismissed their support indicating it amounted to little if any.

The conflict, which bordered on outright dislike, between the two women could perhaps be explored as an outgrowth of the mother-in-law/daughter-in-law relationship coupled with their religious and cultural differences. Kim was bothered by the fact that Emma did not seem accepting of Jewish religious practices. Kim indicated, during the interview, that it bothered her to have her daughters exposed to her non-Jewish mother-in-law. In general, Kim was annoyed by having to care for her mother-in-law and revealed that she never felt close to her. I do, however, feel that much of Kim's frustrations and emotional strain regarding Emma and the situation she found herself in stemmed from the lack of support and communication she received from her husband, Kenny. Communication appeared to be a problem in his family, as we learned that Kim had no idea for years that Emma was married. We also learned that Kenny's siblings were completely out of the picture and offered no assistance, not even the much-needed financial assistance that Kim mentioned. Kim did her best in a situation that afforded her no support, validation, or gratitude. It had to have been difficult to keep up any sort of positive attitude since she did not feel appreciation from her husband or from his mother. She felt they were working against her, not with her.

The chief factor in lessening the burden for Lucille was her realistic, yet responsible, loving, and generous response to the caregiving arrangement in which she found herself. Far from showing any resentment at being burdened with the care of her mentally disadvantaged aunt, Lucille expressed appreciation for the satisfaction her mother drew from having her sister with her. She acknowledged that her role as a caregiver placed limitations on her freedom and resulted in her giving up things that she would like to do; however, she also saw what she was doing as important, and that caregiving had a lot of pluses and very few negatives, saying that she had a lot of good, supportive friends and that she felt wonderful helping her mother. Admitting to occasional burden, she said she got upset when she was forced to recognize, and found it hard to accept, symptoms of further decline in her mother's condition. Even though Lucille was alone in the house with two elderly care-receivers, she referred to having lots of supportive friends. Although Edith's fragile condition prevented her from sharing many activities, Lucille was able to enjoy such give-and-take as teasing, playing little jokes on her, surprising her with pretty things, and taking her out to dinner. The two also shared books and puzzles, watched TV, shared an occasional glass of wine, or just talked. Lucille said that their relationship had improved during the time that her mother had been with her. Though Edith had remembered better times and quite naturally wished her situation could be different with more freedom, mobility, and independence, she showed no suggestion of resentment or bitterness toward her daughter for any form of negative influence on her quality of life because of the strong relationship they shared. On the contrary, she expressed gratitude for the care she received and the wish that she could be less of a burden.

Both Emma and Edith felt dependent and would rather live on their own, but both realized they were not capable of doing so. Emma felt no sense of freedom. She felt demoralized and concerned about her living situation. She indicated that because of the conflict over religion, her daughter-in-law no longer bought her gifts. She felt dissatisfied with her relationship with Kim and with the shared-residence situation in general. Kim being an in-law and the conflict over religion may have contributed to the dissatisfaction. Emma shared no sense of family orientation, affection, give-and-take, activities, or closeness with Kim. She felt as if she contributed to the household by performing tasks that she felt good about, but she did not feel appreciated for her efforts.

Edith was very happy with her situation, even though she, at times, thought about living independently. She felt good that she could help her sister (a member of the household) with cognitive functioning, while her sister was able, in turn, to help Edith with some physical functioning, since Edith was frail from her osteoarthritis. This arrangement gave her a sense of being needed. Edith said she tried to help out and was very concerned about tying down her daughter and keeping her from an active life. She and her daughter shared a strong sense of family orientation, affection, and closeness, and they enjoyed shared activities.

The differences in the dynamics of these two households were so extensive and so complex that they could be adequately approached only through the in-depth interviews to understand the interpersonal relationships versus outward appearances of two women caring for aging family members who had some health concerns and frailties but were still fairly high functioning, both physically and cognitively. Through the interviews, it became clear that the differences in burden were primarily a matter of the differences in the relationships, communication, sense of family, values, and attitudes of the people, not the needs of the care-receivers or the demands of the situations involved.

Chapter Five

A Genuine Valuing of the Mother/Daughter Relationship

Of the ten households involved in the interviews, only the two mother/ daughter pairs in this chapter appeared to be completely satisfied with the shared household caregiving arrangement. After interviewing the two pairs, it became clear to me that they were atypical, even though the mothers had various health conditions and needed assistance with several activities of daily living. What made these mother/daughter pairs different from the other eight?

The biggest difference, as you will see with Ellen and Mary, the next pair, is that they fulfilled something in each other. Yes, they were mother and daughter, but they were friends as well. They truly enjoyed being together, and they each needed the other.

ELLEN AND MARY

Ellen

Sixty-four-year-old Ellen was widowed, worked full-time, had satisfactory health (she had cancer that was controlled and in remission), had no support from either inside or outside the house, and had been caring for her eighty-year-old mother, Mary, for five years. Ellen had not expected to become a caregiver, but she was happy about the arrangement since she was lonely. Finances were not a problem in this household. Her mother only needed some mild, occasional assistance with activities of daily living and had no problems with cognitive functioning. They were the only two who lived in the home and felt that their shared space afforded them the necessary privacy they both appreciated.

Ellen described how she feels about the situation: "I'm real happy with the situation. I like having someone here with me. You can't just live with anybody. I mean it would be hard to find someone to live together with and get along and everything. I would be awfully lonely. I don't like being alone. I never did."

Ellen talked about the emotional uplifts and satisfactions she receives from having her mother with her: "She goes with me most of the time when we go places. I do all the cleaning, and try to keep the house up nice and stuff. I want to do whatever I can to help her. I have no resentment or anything like that. It makes me feel good when I can do something for her. When I can help. I take her blood pressure for her every day. She's always real anxious to get that done. It makes me feel good when I can do those things."

Ellen talked about the give-and-take that they have and how her mother does nice things for her as well: "She has supper ready for me whenever I come home. She makes phone calls for me. She wants things to do. She doesn't want to just sit. I don't know what I'd do with working and everything. It just helps me a lot. She does things for me. Special things for me. Like if I say I'm hungry for something and she goes and fixes it. We've probably gotten closer than we were before."

Ellen and Mary enjoyed sharing activities together, which is no surprise for this relationship.

Ellen continued, "We work on our quilts or watch TV together sometimes. We like to travel. We get in the car and go. We'll go out in the country and check on the crops or whatever, and run our errands around town. We do a lot of that. Just runnin' around. We love to play cards."

A number of studies have interviewed elderly parent and adult child pairs to examine the factors that contribute to quality relationships. Results of one study showed that parents and adult children who had similar values, realistic perceptions of each other, and mutual trust and respect gave the quality of their relationship a high rating,[1] whereas low ratings signified reduced mutual esteem and fewer shared values. Another study interviewed 141 caregiving daughters and their elderly mothers concerning the costs and benefits of caregiving.[2] In general, the costs (negatives) of caregiving were minimized when there was a good relationship between the daughter and her mother. Another study noted in their interviews with 29 pairs of aging mothers and caregiving daughters, that almost half of the relationships were characterized by the joint satisfactions they received.[3] There was little, if any, conflict in their relationship, and there was concern on the part of both daughter and mother for each other's well-being. In addition, both found shared activities to be satisfying and rewarding. The mother/daughter pairs in these studies are very similar to the relationship that Ellen and Mary shared.

Mary

Mary was eighty years old, had high physical and cognitive functioning, and had sufficient income to meet her needs. She indicated that she was very pleased about living with her daughter and thought it was a practical arrangement, since they both had become widows and were lonely. Her health conditions included high blood pressure and arthritis. Mary was still able to drive, however, her driving was basically limited to trips to the grocery store, which was just a few blocks away. She also made phone calls for her daughter and prepared dinner for both of them.

Mary spoke about their relationship and how they felt about one another. We can see from the following statements that there is a lot of balance in this relationship, where they are each dependent on the other in different ways and for different reasons.

Mary had this to say: "I think I feel close at all times. I sort of feel we couldn't get along without each other, because we each, in our own way, are dependent on the other. I think there is a lot of love there. We're very concerned about each other. I'm sure of that."

Here, again, we see the give-and-take that occurs in their relationship and that it makes Mary feel valued and needed.

"I like to do anything I'm able to do," Mary continued. "I always try to have the evening meal ready. It's harder for her to come in after a day's work. I feel that I'm of some use."

Mary described some of the activities they enjoy together: "We like to go places together. We like about the same things, like a picnic together. We enjoy company. We love cards."

Note: When I tried to contact Ellen and Mary for the ten-year follow-up interview, I had learned that Ellen and her mother were both no longer living. My grandmother knew Ellen and Mary, and she had heard that Ellen's cancer had returned. You may recall that Ellen had cancer that was in remission. I am not certain of any other details, except that they both had died. I was saddened by this news. They were both such lovely women. I actually knew Mary when I was very young because she had made my First Communion dress.

ALICE AND BERNICE

Alice

Alice was widowed, worked full-time, was in very good health, and had three children aged twenty-four, twenty-two, and twelve. Alice did not reveal her age. Alice had been sharing a residence with her eighty-seven-year-old mother, Bernice, for one year. I did not interview the children, but they did share with me, informally, that they needed their grandmother more than she needed them. It appeared that they felt good about having their grandmother living with them, and I sensed overall good relationships between the family members. Alice revealed that the two older children run errands for her mother and the youngest child prepares the grandmother's lunch. Alice's mother reciprocates by baby-sitting the twelve-year-old when he comes home from school to ease Alice's mind while she is still at work. Bernice had fairly high physical functioning and no problems with cognitive functioning. Finances were not a problem in this household.

The main theme for this household was one of reciprocity (give-and-take) between the mother and daughter. The reciprocity was possible because there was also mutual trust and respect, punctuated with good communication. Studies have firmly established that the majority of older adults are a part of family networks and that intergenerational reciprocity is strong among most family units.[4] When family members are able to engage in rewarding activities and minimize negative activities, then the multigenerational household can be a satisfactory arrangement.[5] It is worthy to note that it is important not only for caregiving daughters but also for their aging mothers to perceive reciprocity. A give-and-take between the two does not have to be equal. The important point is the perception that there is a give-and-take and that each is contributing in a genuine and caring way.

Alice talked about how her mother, Bernice, alleviates her concerns: "The only thing is that I would be more responsible for my twelve-year-old son and concerned about him when I'm not here. So she is definitely a benefit at relieving my frustrations and my concerns about him. If she would go back [to where she used to live], I don't know what I would do for my son. I really don't. Also, I get frustrated sometimes with the children. She is a sounding board for me."

When I asked Alice whether there was anything she found difficult about caring for her mother, she replied: "The thing that's hard is just trying to arrange a schedule. To get her appointments for the doctor, or whatever. The timing, it's just plain working out the timing. It's not a hardship or anything. It's just plain working around a schedule. I do the same things as what if she weren't here."

Alice's comments really emphasize the need she has for her mother and the give-and-take that occurs between the two: "I love it. It's the best of all worlds. It's nice having her presence in the house for everybody. I don't know what I'd do if she weren't here now. I mean I really don't. We've talked about it. I don't think she understands how much she really is a help."

Alice and Bernice were friends as much as they were mother and daughter. Alice said, "We enjoy lunch together, TV, conversations, laughing, and we do a lot of that. I enjoy these activities just because I enjoy having her here. I enjoy doing things with her. We've always enjoyed each other. We just have a closeness all the time. We've had some real laughs. Things that have happened to us that we can't explain to anyone. We still sit and laugh. Just, you know, special things. I just enjoy having her here. I have the feelings that I'm glad she's here, but not that I could do anything for her (to make me feel good). Just the natural flow."

Mary and Bernice

The mothers in both of the mother/daughter pairs derived just as much pleasure and satisfaction from the shared-residence situation as did their daughters. Both mothers' characterizations of the relationship were similar to their daughters' representation of the relationship. It appears that, like their daughters, both Mary and Bernice had their own coping skills, realistic solutions, and a positive attitude. Both mothers felt that they were a part of a close family.

Both mothers indicated that they had no worries or concerns about living with their daughters. When asked about feeling dissatisfied, they both said they "never" felt that way. If they did, they each had their solutions. Mary said that if she ever felt dissatisfied or unhappy she just got into her car and went for a change of atmosphere. Bernice said that if she ever were to feel dissatisfied she would just go back home, to where she lived prior to moving in with her daughter. Alice, her daughter, however, did not feel her mother could live on her own. Privacy, loneliness, and threatened reciprocity were not problems for either Mary or Bernice. However, Bernice did say that she missed her friends and meeting new people in the out-of-state housing complex where she used to live.

While Mary was aware that she depended on Ellen, her daughter, Mary also knew that Ellen depended on Mary as well. Bernice talked about the fact that she came from a close family, and she had raised her children to be the same way. Both mothers knew they were appreciated and welcome, and each felt that they were contributing to the household. The number of tasks they performed was not important, but the feeling that they were adding to the household was. Actual physical demonstration of affection was not a large part of these two relationships, but a genuine caring and closeness was evident.

Alice and Bernice: Ten Years Later

Jeanne: *How long after the interview, ten years ago, did you continue caring for your mother here in your home?*

Alice: I cared for her for about six years. She was in the hospital, and what happened is she was lacking oxygen; we put her in the care center thinking she would not survive. We didn't think she was going to live that long. Then they started giving her oxygen. She was on oxygen for about six months. She was in a wheelchair because of her back. One time she fell in the kitchen, and then we knew she really couldn't be by herself. She was fine until then.

Jeanne: *Why did you decide to stop caring for her here?*

Alice: We just had to do what was available. I had worked and I knew a lot of the people out there. There was no way we could bring her home at the time. We thought we were going to lose her. She was not in a stable condition at all. So, she really knew she had to go. Really, there was not that much discussion about it.

Jeanne: *How was the decision made to have your mother cared for elsewhere? How did you decide where?*

Alice: She was really acceptable to it. She was really open to anything that ever happened. You know she was just like, "it happens." She would laugh a lot, and the kids would go in and spend time with her and just laugh. She was very acceptable to the situation. She didn't want it to happen but she knew. We really didn't talk about it that much.

Jeanne: *Did the quality of your relationship change in any way as your mother's health began to further deteriorate? If so, in what way?*

Alice: She just lived it up until the day she died. She did everything until she died. The only thing is that she was more tired, and she would lie down and I saw that. See the day she died she had gone down for lunch. She was talking with everyone, and then went in for a nap and just never woke up.

Jeanne: *Did the quality of the relationship you shared with your mother help or hinder your decision to no longer provide care here?*

Alice: I really had no choice, for her age and not being able to take care of herself. I couldn't find any dependable people, and then she got very sick. She was just screaming and imagining things. And that was because of the lack of oxygen.

Jeanne: *In what way did the household functioning change as the result of the change in your mother's health and residence?*

Alice: I never really paid attention that much, because we still went out there a lot and still did all her laundry and I still did a lot of her caregiving there. It was even more so with her not being here, because I was always having to run out there.

Jeanne: *So, it wasn't like there was all this empty space?*

Alice: No, because all of mother's things were still here. I never did anything. I never took her things out of the closet. I just took things out to her.

Jeanne: *Was the household different here, because you said you were always busy going there?*

Alice: I didn't really ever think about it, to tell you the truth. It was just another step and that is what you do, and I was always going to bring her home. And then that just did not happen.

Jeanne: *Was accepting the death of your mother more difficult because of the relationship you shared?*

Alice: Yeah, because it's funny because this last fall was the hardest, a year after she had died. And I had so much going on that all of a sudden everything was just there. I quit my job in February a year ago; I was to the point I couldn't go anymore. And then I started to miss her. I said, you know I didn't realize how much I missed her until my sister and I started to talk about it, and I missed her. I was so in the middle of doing stuff that I didn't feel it. It was also the anniversary of my husband's death, during the week after the funeral. So, it didn't catch up with me until a year later on my birthday and then a year after her death, Thanksgiving. My kids are gone now, and so I spend a lot of time by myself.

Jeanne: *Was there a sense of loss, or was there a sense of relief after your mother's death? If so, in what way?*

Alice: Relief, not really, but I didn't know what to do. I had a loss; it's a different type of loss. Not having someone need me anymore.

Jeanne: *In what way did the household functioning change as the result of your mother's absence?*

Alice: I changed jobs in there, too. See, Mother was there for my son, when I wasn't here. I can't really, I don't know because my son was here and I could have her help. The focus just changed to being out there [the care facility] instead of here. My mother was so with it, that's why I tried to get her at a meal table [at the facility] with people that could talk with her.

Jeanne: *Looking back to ten years ago and thinking about now, has your perception of the caregiving situation changed in any way? If so, in what way?*

Alice: It was the best thing I ever did. It was wonderful for me and wonderful for the children. It was positive for everyone in all the ways. Never a negative from any of the three children she was with.

Jeanne: *Looking back to ten years ago and thinking about now, has your perception of your relationship with your mother changed in any way? If so, in what way?*

Alice: No, it has always been the same. I just never thought of it differently. In the real world, I have no regrets at all. I don't mean to make it so positive, but there wasn't anything that was negative. And I say that, with my husband, we had a very good marriage. He died of a heart attack. We always saw the positives. My mother lived to be ninety-five. And she just lay down and never woke up.

DISCUSSION OF INITIAL INTERVIEWS

It appeared that one of the factors resulting in the low level of perceived burden and high degree of satisfaction experienced by both the daughters and the mothers in the two households was reciprocity. There was a sense of balance, of give-and-take, of pulling together as a family unit, and of moving in the "natural flow" of living together. It was not that the mothers did so much more for the daughters, or that they tried to give as much as they received, but it was that they were a part of a family, rather than intruders. There was a history of a strong relationship that continued through their lives, on into a shared-residence caregiving situation. The daughters accepted the situation as if it were the natural and obvious arrangement. The daughters and their mothers were sources of comfort for each other, whether it was to alleviate loneliness or lessen any concerns for one another. Ellen spoke of the fact that her mother made important phone calls for her during the day while she was at work, ran errands for her, and had dinner waiting on the table when she got home. Alice discussed the importance of having her mother there to "relieve frustrations and concerns" about her twelve-year-old son by being with him while she was working. Both daughters commented that they did not know what they would do without their mothers and that they had grown closer as a result of living together.

In both households, the daughters and their mothers enjoyed sharing a variety of activities. Other households that were experiencing more burden either did not enjoy a variety of activities with their mothers, or felt obligated to do things with their mothers, or did not enjoy their mother's company. The fact that both Ellen and Alice were widows suggests a need they had for a support person, as well as a valuing of their mother as that person. In any event, there was a high level of reciprocity. Both Mary and Bernice needed assistance with several activities of daily living, but both were mentally competent and able to contribute to the relationship. Bernice had a physical functioning level similar to that of four other mothers who participated in the interviews who were in households where their daughters had reported a high degree of feeling burdened. Mary's physical functioning was similar to one other mother who participated in the interviews and, yet, had a daughter who did not have a good relationship with her mother (Kate and Margaret). The functioning level of Mary and Bernice contributed to the satisfaction in the households, permitting considerable independence. In some of the more burdened households, part of the frustration the daughters felt was due to the lack of a give-and-take mother/daughter relationship and the lack of quality interactions. Some daughters missed what they once shared with their mothers, and some daughters longed for what they had never had.

Chapter Six

Mother and Daughter Relationship Quality

It appeared that the main element in accounting for the differences in the level of burden or satisfaction the daughters in these families experienced was the perception of the relationship quality between themselves and their mothers. Getting both the perspective of the daughters and their mothers allowed for greater insight into the dynamics involved in the relationship. Lois, Natalie, Lucille, Tammy, Ellen, and Alice all experienced rich relationships with their mothers, characterized by feelings of closeness, a sense of family orientation, reciprocity, communication, and compassion. These elements appeared to be not as strong or were mostly absent for Kate, Kim, Janice, and Lillian.

Lois, who was the 81-year-old daughter caring for her 104-year-old mother, had a relationship with her mother based on a sense of responsibility, duty, and family. Natalie was retired and caring for her mother who had suffered a stroke. Her relationship was grounded in activities enjoyed together, a strong sense of family, and feelings of closeness. Lucille was caring for both her mother and her aunt. The foundations for the relationship with her mother were affection, shared activities, a high level of communication, a strong sense of family, high reciprocity, and emotional support. Tammy, the niece caring for her aunt, found that the bases for a quality relationship were excellent communication and a sense of family.

Kate, Kim, Janice, and Lillian all, to varying degrees, reported poor relationships with either their spouses, their children, or their mothers, or some combination of the three. Kate was a prisoner to her own "perfectionism" and had a daughter who was incompatible with both her mother and grandmother. Kate also felt obligated to be at home when she wasn't at work. Kim had a religious conflict with her mother-in-law and frequent disagreements with her spouse concerning her care and treatment of his mother. She indicated that, while her mother-in-law was around, she did not feel free to do what she wanted or have the freedom to just be herself. Janice described her mother as selfish and controlling. She talked about how unpleasant it was to experience the role reversal where she was the parent and her mother was the child and how upsetting it was to have all the old conflicts from her childhood come flooding to the surface. Everyone in the family was concerned on a daily basis about what kind of mood the care-receiver would be in, wondering if she would disrupt a family activity, such as dinner, by her behavior. Amelia, the mother, had her concerns as well. She indicated that she did not feel free to play her music as loudly as she wanted to. She felt that she did not have the privacy and freedoms that she had when she was living with her husband. Lillian, whose spouse had a very poor relationship with Lillian's mother, described her mother as selfish and demanding. In these households, relationship quality was thwarted by conflicts between family members, lack of communication, lack of family orientation and closeness, limited sharing of activities, and a limited degree of reciprocity.

Many of the daughters, whether they had good relationships with their mothers or not, were affected by their mother's impact on house-hold functioning—having to make special arrangements or do special planning for activities; having to witness, on a day-to-day basis, the deterioration of their mother's health; and dealing with old emotions and past memories concerning their relationship with their mother. Several of the daughters identified role reversal as troubling.

The mothers in the households were affected in the areas of role loss, loss of privacy, loss of independence, and, for some, demoralization of having to be dependent upon others. Several mothers disclosed that thinking back to their life when they had a spouse and their own home was emotionally difficult for them. They longed for their former life and independence.

It appeared that conflicts and (in some cases) role reversal, the functioning level of the mother, and lack of privacy contributed to strained relations between mothers and daughters. However, the importance of these factors is limited to the extent that they affected those households where relationship quality was already low. These factors themselves did not appear to be the cause of poor relations in those households.

The shared-household caregiving situation brought to the surface emotions that caregivers had long thought to be in the past; emotions involving memories of their interactions and conflicts with their parent. It is that history of a poor relationship that contributed to a negative shared-household situation. Many of the daughters were caring for mothers with multiple physical health conditions, and a couple of the mothers had some cognitive impairments that ranged from mild confusion to depression; however, even comparing across households where the mothers' health conditions were similarly impaired, the mother's compromised health status did not account for why relationship quality was strong or conflicted.

Even in the households where daughters reported feeling burdened, satisfaction came from feeling good about providing care. Daughters felt that, in the absence of anyone else to provide care, they were needed and that they were giving good care. From the ten-year follow-up interviews, we heard that they had no regrets and that they would not go back and change anything because they did the best they could.

Primarily, mothers felt satisfaction in areas similar to those that were satisfying to their daughters. The more satisfied households were happy about a good relationship between mother and daughter, good communication, reciprocity, feelings of closeness, shared activities, receiving gifts, and a sense of truly being wanted and needed.

LIFE AFTER CAREGIVING: THEMES FROM THE TEN-YEAR FOLLOW-UP INTERVIEWS

Seven daughters participated in the ten-year follow-up interviews. Of the seven, five of them indicated that their mothers were no longer living, and two of them had to put their mothers in long-term care. I was unable to locate two daughters who had participated in the initial interviews, and one mother/daughter pair had both passed away. The interviews with seven of the ten adult daughters had varied responses to the set questions I posed; however, a thorough analysis revealed eight common themes that distinctly emerged from the interview data:

- I would not go back and change anything.
- I did the best I could.
- I had no regrets.
- I had no choice.
- I did what I had to do.
- I felt a sense of relief.
- I feel lonely and have a sense of loss: how do I spend my time?
- Perceptions, overall, were more positive upon reflection.

It appears to be human nature to reflect back on the past and our experiences with our loved ones as being positive—perhaps even more so than was actually felt at the time. In several of the interviews, the adult daughters talked about how unresolved conflicts and issues they had encountered with their mother, when they were younger, had come back now that they were living together. In the ten-year follow-up interviews, however, when asked about unresolved conflicts, the replies were quite similar. Daughters who had initially reported conflicts with their mother were now indicating that they did not have any conflicts, nor had they ever had conflicts with their mother. There was a tendency to reflect back on the relationship as being more positive than it actually had been reported ten years prior. The daughters were now ten years older, and perhaps they were more keenly aware of their own mortality and had reached a new level of understanding about what it means to grow older. It appeared that there were more positive reflections on the caregiving relationship; the daughters felt they had made an important contribution to the life of their mother, had done something of significance and of value, and had successfully navigated and emerged from a difficult situation. Whatever the actual reasons were for feeling good about having provided care to their mothers, this is an important finding that daughters find meaning from the mother/daughter caregiving relationship, regardless of how difficult the journey.

LOOKING AHEAD

The mother/daughter caregiving relationship is not a collection of various factors of burden or satisfaction. It is a dynamic and interactive relationship with a history as well as current circumstances. If the quality of the relationship between mothers and daughters is critical to the nature of burden and satisfaction in the caregiving arrangement, particularly in the day-to-day ongoing situation of shared-residence caregiving, then more than adult day care, home-delivered meals, case management, and the support of family and friends are necessary for comprehensive, effective assistance for mother/daughter caregiving situations. Possible support could come from the reinforcement and encouragement of caregiver support groups, family counselors, and mental health therapists. Such intervention would assist mothers and daughters with poor relationships in restoring, improving, and cultivating communication and lessening conflicts. However, it is unrealistic to assume that all mothers and daughters who have low-quality relationships can overcome lifetimes of problems through the aid of a therapist or service provider. The decision to live together is a big step, and as you read from our ten families, it can be a very rewarding experience, where you have the chance to bond and get to know each other in a new way, or it can be a time of frustration and conflict. Either way, it is best to go into it by first having talked through it together realistically and honestly.

Chapter Seven

Realistic Considerations about Living Together

Living with your parent can be seen as an opportunity to bond and a chance for you to reconnect in new ways. No matter how close and loving your relationship may be, the dynamics of the relationship and the entire household can change. As we heard from one family member in a previous chapter, having their grandmother come live with them "changes not what you do, but how you relate to what you are doing." That included eating dinner, getting up in the morning, going to bed, and everything in between. Lifestyles of families may be upended, personalities may clash, and schedules might conflict. The journey will be smoother if you and your loved one navigate this very emotional decision of living together by thinking through the pros and cons. Each family will have its own reasons for wanting (or not wanting) to take such a step.

You may decide that a move is right because your parent can no longer manage their own home. It is important to learn as much as you can about various living arrangements before making the decision with your parent about what is best. Perhaps you know what might be best for your parent, but you might not be the person with the decision-making authority or your parent refuses to see that they are no longer in a situation that is a viable and safe option for them.

Keep in mind that leaving a home, community, and familiar medical care can be very disruptive and difficult for your older parent, especially if they are not looking forward to the change. You might first want to explore what services are available in your parents' community to help them in their home, such as home health care, housekeeping, personal care, and transportation services.

Families must think carefully before moving an aging parent into an adult child's home, and both you and your parent must ask yourselves how you feel about the possibility of a new living arrangement. There are a lot of questions to consider. Here are some good examples:

- Is there space in your home? Can some space be converted to make room?
- Is your home a safe space, or do you need to make some changes/ upgrades to make it safe?
- Are there children/teens present in your home? Do they have a good relationship with your parent?
- Do you have past unresolved conflicts with your parent? How well do you communicate?
- Are there pets in your home?
- How will finances be handled? Should your parent pay some living expenses?
- Is there someone available during the day to help your older parent?
- Will you need to alter your work schedule to accommodate your parent?
- What is your parent able to do for themselves? How much help will your parent need?
- What personal care are you willing and able to provide? For example, will you be able to move your parent from a chair to a bed or toilet, change adult diapers, or deal with a feeding tube?
- What kinds of home care services are available in your community?
- Have you located other services that your parent may need (e.g., banking, counseling, pharmacy, senior center, adult day care, or church or synagogue)?
- What kind of specialized medical care is available or nearby?
- How do the other family members living in the home feel about the possibility of your parent coming to live in their home? (Everyone should be allowed to give input.)
- Will everyone have enough privacy? How will you set and maintain boundaries?

Studies have found that "caregivers in a joint living situation are always 'on call,' with a resulting loss of privacy, autonomy, and sleep. In contrast, caring for an older person who lives separately requires managing two households."[1] Caregivers who have their parents living with them report higher levels of psychological stress, increased demands on physical space, and loss of personal freedom.[2] They also are more likely to use psychotropic drugs, report higher levels of stress symptoms, and report the lowest levels of life satisfaction. Additionally, caregivers in shared-residence situations are considerably worse off in the areas of mental health and social participation with other family members and friends.[3] Conversely, the multigenerational household caregiving arrangement can have positive consequences that can be perceived as rewarding and as an opportunity by both the caregiver and the aging parent. For example, some of the benefits can be inexpensive child care, increased income to the family, and companionship for the multiple generations.[4] Families need to consider the benefits in relation to any negative impact the presence of an aging parent may have on the overall household; families must also examine how a shared-living arrangement may affect their parent. A positive relationship with the ability to work through conflict will go a long way in creating a satisfying shared-residence household.

One of the most important points to remember is that open communication with your parent and your other family members who are living at home is key. Everyone should be allowed to talk about hopes, fears, concerns, and expectations. You might decide to try it for six months or a year. The other reality may be that this is the only viable option. In this case, you will have to be aware that you really don't know how long your parent may be living with you or how their health may change over the duration of their stay, but at least you can go into it with some idea of the kinds of things to consider. Deciding to have your parent come to live with you is not about a collection of factors or having the right answers to a series of questions, it is about your relationship with your parent and the people in your life and about your current circumstances. Sometimes the only question to answer is this: "What feels right?"[5]

Chapter Eight

Creating Therapy in a Box

If you are providing care for your mother at home, then something you might find very useful is a therapy box. My mother and I made one for my grandmother and found it quite helpful. The various items in a therapy box can assist with promoting communication, mild physical therapy, memory enhancement, and the sharing of activities for interaction. You can easily put together your own therapy box, and the items are easily accessible and relatively inexpensive. You can customize your own box based on your parent's specific interests. Here is what my mother and I included in our therapy box for my grandmother.

THERAPY-IN-A-BOX ITEMS

- Medium-sized plastic container or box (You can decorate it or put your mother's name on it.)
- Adult coloring book
- Box of crayons
- Magazines
- Crossword puzzle books
- Pretty paper/cards/envelopes/stamps (for letter writing to friends/family)
- Playdough or Floam (You can "hide" marbles inside for your parent to find/pick out, which is great therapy for hand strength and coordination.)

- Rock painting kit (We found one at Walmart.)
- Puzzles with big pieces (We used a puzzle of the fifty states and then asked my grandmother to put in the puzzle pieces of the states she has visited. We then asked her to put in the puzzle pieces of the states she would have liked to have visited.)
- Soft bouncy ball that's big enough to toss back and forth (A ball is great for coordination and muscle toning.)
- Stretchy fitness bands to pull on for strength building
- Cake/brownie/cookie mix (You can have your parent stir up the ingredients; it's a nice activity to do together.)
- Photo album filled with pictures
- Old recipe book to spark memories of favorite recipes your parent once prepared
- Hand/body lotion (This relieves dry skin but also promotes touch. I would rub lotion on my grandmother's face, arms, and hands.)
- Memory prompt questions (My grandmother often liked to tell a story from her childhood about when she and her parents and baby brother were in a horse-and-buggy accident. We asked her memory prompt questions to promote her talking about it: Who was in the buggy? How old were you? How did you get thrown out of the buggy? Who found you? How did your family get help?)
- Board game
- Favorite book (perhaps a book about birds, poetry, history)
- CD or sheet music to a favorite song

You can add anything to the therapy box that will promote enjoyment or be something positive for the two of you to do together. Your parent might feel too overwhelmed to select something on their own from the entire therapy box, so you can put instructions on index cards. Your parent can select a card that will tell them what to do. For example, one index card might say, "Have you had your water today? Drink, drink drink!" Others might say, "Color a page from the coloring book," "Toss the ball back and forth ten times," or "Wash your hands and put on hand cream."

The purpose of the therapy in a box is to take a little pressure off of you to think of things to do, and each item in the box is something positive—whether it is promoting coordination and strength, memory enhancement, hydration, relaxation, communication between you and your parent, or just sharing an enjoyable activity. You might even want to occasionally hide little surprises in the box your parent can discover—a candy bar, a piece of fruit, a new pair of slipper socks, or a scarf. Just be creative and have fun with your therapy in a box. You can customize it to whatever works for you and your parent.

Pinterest.com has some very creative and inexpensive ideas for creating a "dementia busy box" and other kinds of memory aids. You can also find ideas for creating puzzles, games, and activities for your parent.

PET THERAPY

We all know the joy of caring for a beloved pet, however, there are issues and hazards to consider: your parent might possibly trip over a pet, pets require exercise and potty breaks, and pet food and veterinary care are expensive. One idea is to purchase a lifelike pet, with built-in sensors that respond to motion and touch. Ageless Innovations sells cats for a little over $100 (Robotshop.com) and they look, feel, and sound like a real cat. They respond to petting, hugging, and motion. For example, if you pet the cat's left cheek, it will nuzzle its head into your hand. You can purchase a Tabby Cat or a Silver and White Cat. They are for older adults with or without dementia and come with a five-star rating. I actually purchased one of these cats and donated it to a local memory care facility, so I have had the opportunity to experience firsthand what it is like to interact with this very high-quality type of pet. I also purchased a small cat bed for "Joan" (I named her) so that she had her own place to sleep at the facility!

CARING FOR PLANTS

A plant or two is a wonderful way to brighten up any living space, and research has proven that caring for plants can reduce stress levels as well as blood pressure. Plants can also improve the air quality in your home. Some easy-to-care-for houseplants for older adults are Cast Iron Plant, Devil's Ivy, Peace Lilies, Spider Plant, and Mother-in-Law's Tongue. If your loved one once enjoyed gardening and/or landscaping, consider building a raised garden box out on the patio, deck, or in the yard. A raised garden box is one that your parent can easily reach without having to bend over, and it is small enough to be cared for without your parent feeling overwhelmed. You can also plant tomato plants, peppers, or other easy-to-grow vegetables in pots. It can be very rewarding to plant flowers and vegetables and watch them grow, and it will give your parent a sense of accomplishment and something to look forward to each day.

Chapter Nine

Inheriting Memories

In my discussions of the mother and daughter pairs, I often mentioned the importance of shared activities, and reminiscence is certainly an activity that not only can be shared but also is valuable to all who participate. Reminiscence is the review of past experiences. It is something in which we all can engage. It can bring peace and resolution to older people as they find meaning in their memories. In later years, people can come to terms with events and feelings they may not have had time to reflect upon and think through when they occurred. The opportunity to reminisce can help your parent unlock what may be long forgotten resources within themselves. Remembering a time when they felt strong or capable or when they overcame problems, made difficult choices, or dealt with losses can again fill them with a sense of power and competency.

Research has shown that older people who undergo life review are less withdrawn and apathetic. Reminiscing promotes mental and emotional well-being and combats isolation, loneliness, and depression. The process helps older people get back in touch with things that matter to them.

Reminiscing with your parent can help bring you closer together because it shows you are interested in your parent, and if the memory is one that you both remember, it helps establish a sense of closeness.

The benefits of reminiscence are many. People who reminisce together

- Create a sense of continuity, linking accomplishments of the past to the present

- Discover interesting things about each other or a period of history
- Transmit cultural heritage
- Communicate family folklore
- Build self-esteem
- Resolve conflict and/or fears
- Reflect and reassess life achievements
- Promote intergenerational understanding
- Decrease isolation
- Increase social interaction

Certain words, smells, sounds, objects, or music can spark memories. We all know that feeling of hearing a song or smelling a certain scent, and suddenly we are right back "in the moment."

Consider the following, and perhaps you can try a few of these with your parent:

- Photographs (focus on personal photos or those from the period being recalled)
- Memorabilia (anything from a handmade quilt or a special plate or dish, to a childhood book or toy)
- Historic event (ask questions dealing with a historic event such as the Depression or World War II)
- Family occasions (ask your parent to recollect birthdays, weddings, or other special events)
- Short stories or poems (use short stories or poems about the past)

Reminiscence isn't difficult. In order to make it happen, you just need to be a caring, interested, and sensitive listener. The following are a few tips on how you can help your parent reminisce:

Listen: Sit and face your parent and be sure to maintain eye contact. By maintaining eye contact, you are showing them that you are interested in what they are saying and that you care. When they are talking, use brief responses, such as "Okay" or "I see." Let them know you understand.

Don't rush your parent: If you rush your parent, they may not feel heard or understood. It is important for you not to speak too quickly so that while you and your parent are sharing, they have time to process the conversation.

Ask questions: Asking questions helps clarify what you hear them saying. You can ask questions that begin with the words *what, where, how, when,* or *who.* Try not to ask the question *why* because it requires that the person give a reasoned response and they may not know why. You can ask questions such as "How did you feel when that happened?" or "What was that like?" If you don't know what to say, you can always say, "Tell me more about that."

Dealing with a negative memory: In this case, you may want to say, "I can see how you would feel that way" *not* "I know how you feel." If you say, "I know how you feel," your parent may think, "How can you know how I feel?" Your parent then might close off from you. Try not to judge or criticize.

What to do if your parent repeats themselves: How many times have you thought to yourself, *I have heard this same story a hundred times. I have no patience or time for this! Why does my parent tell this story, and countless others, over and over?* Then, of course, you feel guilty about being frustrated and angry. Sometimes you may wonder, "Why is my mother telling the same story?" You might even feel worried that this is a sign of mental deterioration, and your frustration is really fear that your mother is starting to show signs of dementia.

Stories that are often repeated by older people are actually positive attempts to make sense of or resolve an important conflict in their lives. In addition to resolving conflict, older adults may repeat the same stories to resolve anger from a past event or situation. They may be trying to work through some grief, or they want to recapture a special moment or important event. In order to deal with and understand when your parent is repeating themselves, try asking more questions about the event. For example: Who else was present? Were they supportive? What else was going on in your life at the time? In addition, try changing the topic for a few minutes each time. You could suggest doing an activity together. Start each conversation with a new topic and then let your parent repeat their story. Sometimes just having someone to listen and be supportive can help the person to stop wanting to repeat their story.[1]

Here are some active listening techniques to help you in reminiscing with your parent:[2]

- Pay attention to nonverbal language. Body language gives important clues to attitudes and feelings. Notice posture, gestures, facial expressions, and eye contact.

- Gain the person's attention. Sit in front of and at the same level as your parent and maintain eye contact.
- If they hear you but don't completely understand you, just rephrase your statement or question.
- Concentrate and work at listening; it's hard work. If your mind wanders and you lose attention and/or patience, try to come back to the task at hand. Your parent will notice if you are listening, and it will matter to them that you are trying and that you care.
- If they grope for words, gently provide assistance.
- Use simple, direct wording when responding back to them. Present one question or statement at a time. Otherwise, they might feel overwhelmed.
- Avoid the temptation to jump into the conversation with stories and examples of your own.
- Be empathetic. Put yourself in their shoes. Imagine how they might be feeling or thinking.
- Guard against asking questions that may get the speaker off track.

There are lots of journals you can pick up at the bookstore where your parent can respond to question prompts and then fill in their memory. Here are some questions to help you get started:

What is your earliest memory?
What are some of your favorite childhood memories?
Tell me about pets you had as a child.
What did you like about school?
Who was your favorite teacher?
Who were your friends?
What were your favorite foods as a child?
Tell me about your first job.
What was dating like?
What first attracted you to the person you married?
What was the most interesting period of history you lived through?
What is the biggest difference between your childhood and that of your
    children? Grandchildren?

These are just some of the questions you can ask, and these questions may lead to more memories!

Chapter Ten

Handling Memory Loss

Several daughters in the previous chapters on mother/daughter caregiving described their mothers as having some issues with depression. I thought it might be important to include a chapter on depression and how to know what the signs of depression are versus the signs of dementia. Also, memory loss can occur in both depression and dementia, so I have included a discussion of memory loss. Seeing any kind of decline in your parent's memory, other than some typical age-related changes of not recalling names, faces, and places as easily, can be terrifying. If you can, with the assistance of your parent's doctor, begin to examine the things that are treatable; it might be helpful. My mother is seventy-six years old, and a few years ago she had a dramatic change in her personality. She was crying all the time, paranoid, and accusatory, and she was also experiencing weight gain, hair loss, and dry skin. I only noticed the personality changes, and it almost ruined our relationship. For a while, I actually had to stop talking to her because she was so unreasonable. Finally, she admitted she had stopped taking several of her medications, and one of them was her thyroid medication, which is very serious. It took almost two years to get her physical and mental health back on track. Once I understood what was happening, I could have patience and understanding, and I supported her in ensuring she saw her doctor, and she even started going to counseling for some extra assistance. As another example, there have been a couple of times that my grandmother (soon to be 100) has been so dehydrated that she cries, becomes confused, and doesn't feel well, and as soon as my mother and I realize that she has not been drinking enough, we start with the fluids and proper nutrition. On a side note, my grandmother has become very stubborn, and one of the things she does to have control is that she will refuse to eat or drink enough. Managing difficult behaviors is for another chapter!

It is important to note that, of course, dementia is not treatable, but there are some things that can be checked out related to memory loss. Some memory problems are related to health issues that may be treatable. For example, medication side effects; vitamin B12 deficiency; head injury, such as a concussion from a fall or accident; drinking too much alcohol; and tumors, infections, or blood clots in the brain can cause memory loss or possibly dementia. Some thyroid, kidney, or liver disorders also can lead to memory loss. Emotional problems, such as stress, anxiety, or depression, can make a person more forgetful and can be mistaken for dementia. Trying to deal with life changes can leave some people confused and forgetful. If those feelings persist, then treatment may include counseling, medication, or both.

For some older people, memory problems are a sign of mild cognitive impairment, Alzheimer's disease, or a related dementia. Mild Cognitive Impairment (MCI) is a condition where someone has more memory problems than normal for people their age; however, their symptoms are not as severe as those of people with Alzheimer's disease, and they are able to carry out their normal daily activities. Signs of MCI include losing things often, forgetting to go to important events or appointments, and having more trouble coming up with words than other people of the same age. Family and friends may notice memory lapses, and the person with MCI may worry about losing his or her memory. Older adults who are worried about memory problems should see a doctor. Memory loss does not always mean Alzheimer's. There are causes of memory loss that can absolutely be treated. Getting an early and proper diagnosis of memory loss can help you identify any other possible health issues that can be treated.

How can you tell the difference between mild forgetfulness and serious memory problems?[1] Table 10.1 shows a comparison.

Sometimes depression and dementia can look similar, so here is a list of the symptoms for each. It is important to be able to identify which ones you are noticing and then talk with your parent's doctor about what you have observed. I also want to note that it is critical for you

Table 10.1. Normal Aging versus Alzheimer's Disease

Normal Aging	Alzheimer's Disease
Making a bad decision once in a while	Making poor judgments and decisions often
Missing a monthly payment	Problems taking care of monthly bills
Sometimes forgetting which word to use	Trouble having a conversation
Losing things from time to time	Misplacing things often and being unable to find them
Forgetting which day it is but later remembering	Losing track of the date or time of year

to be aware of depression symptoms for yourself. Caregivers are often likely candidates for depression for a variety of reasons. I will address this in a chapter on the importance of taking care of yourself.

SYMPTOMS OF DEPRESSION[2]

- Feeling unhappy most of the time
- Worrying a lot or feeling anxious or panicky
- Getting restless and irritable
- Feeling life is pointless and not worth living
- Getting lonely or bored
- Crying a lot for no apparent reason
- Not caring how you look
- Sleeping too much or too little
- Feeling tired even when you're not doing much
- Finding it a struggle to do simple chores
- Having difficulty remembering things
- Having thoughts of harming yourself
- Finding it hard to make decisions
- Dwelling on things that happened in the past
- Having unexplained aches and pains
- Worrying that you are seriously ill
- Withdrawing from family and friends
- Losing confidence in yourself
- Experiencing a loss of appetite or weight

Depression does not have a single cause. It can be triggered by a life crisis, physical illness, or something else—but it can also occur spontaneously. Scientists believe several factors can contribute to depression:[3]

- **Trauma:** When people experience trauma at an early age, it can cause long-term changes in how their brains respond to fear and stress. These changes may lead to depression.
- **Genetics:** Mood disorders, such as depression, tend to run in families.
- **Personal history and life circumstances:** Marital status, relationship changes, financial standing, and where a person lives influence whether a person develops depression.
- **Brain changes:** Imaging studies have shown that the frontal lobe of the brain becomes less active when a person is depressed.
- **Alcohol misuse:** Alcohol can worsen depressive symptoms.
- **Co-occurring illnesses:** Depression can co-occur with other serious medical illnesses such as diabetes, cancer, heart disease, and Parkinson's disease. Depression can make these conditions worse and vice versa.

Some people are more likely to experience depression. Women are more likely than men to become seriously depressed. Biological factors like hormonal changes may make older women more vulnerable. The stresses of maintaining relationships or caring for an ill loved one and children also typically fall more heavily on women, which could contribute to higher rates of depression. Unmarried and widowed individuals, as well as those who lack supportive social networks, also have elevated rates of depression. There are also health conditions that are known to be associated with the development of depression. This section on depression is vitally important for both you and your parent, and it is important to be aware of the signs and symptoms.

SYMPTOMS OF ALZHEIMER'S DISEASE

- Memory loss that affects day-to-day function
- Difficulty performing familiar tasks
- Problems with language
- Asking the same question or repeating the same story over and over
- Getting confused about time, people, and places

- Becoming lost in familiar places
- Having trouble handling money or paying bills
- Increased anxiety and/or aggression
- Poor or decreased judgment
- Problems with abstract thinking
- Misplacing things
- Changes in mood or behavior
- Changes in personality
- Loss of initiative

As you can see, there are differences between the symptoms of depression and Alzheimer's disease, and mainly the differences are related to memory. While there can be mood changes associated with the symptoms of Alzheimer's disease, this type of dementia is more of a cognitive disorder rather than a mood disorder like depression. Memory problems can also be associated with depression, however, so remember only a medical professional like your parent's doctor can correctly diagnose your parent's symptoms.

TIPS FOR DEALING WITH NORMAL
AGE-RELATED FORGETFULNESS

My mother purchased a small notebook to make notes of each day's tasks and appointments. She even used the notebook with my grandmother to write things down if my grandmother was having a harder time hearing that particular day. My grandmother would also jot down a word or question about various things that cropped up when she was not with my mother, and this way she wouldn't forget what it was she needed to ask.

My mother also purchased a medium-sized chalkboard to put near my grandmother that proved quite helpful for leaving her important notes. When my grandmother would go for a nap, for example, my mother would put the chalkboard beside her bed with a very visible note on it, saying something like, "Don't get up. I will be back at 3:00." In the past, my grandmother would often get up and try to walk across the room and invariably would fall. The chalkboard reminded her not to do that and that my mother would be right back to take care of her needs. My grandmother would instead sit up and get a drink or a snack that my mother had placed on a nearby table and wait for my mother to return. It worked very well; my grandmother was much safer, and it gave my mother peace of mind. The chalkboard was something that could be seen right away, and it worked better than a slip of paper that might be missed.

There are some things that you and your parent can try to help with age-related memory loss:[4]

- Maintaining a healthy weight and eating healthful foods is important. I know it's easier said than done, but obesity is a risk factor for cognitive decline. A healthful diet can help reduce the risk of many chronic diseases and may also help keep your brain healthy.
- Getting enough sleep can improve memory performance.
- Challenging your brain with some memory games and activities, such as crossword puzzles and reading, can assist with reducing your risk of dementia.
- Keeping up interests or hobbies, and developing new ones (such as volunteering and visiting with family and friends) is a great way to stay mentally active.
- Engaging in physical activity and exercise can keep you both cognitively and physically fit. Several studies have associated aerobic exercise (such as brisk walking) with better brain function, although more research is needed to say for sure whether exercise can help prevent or delay dementia. Exercise can also help relieve feelings of stress, anxiety, or depression.
- Limiting alcohol use is always a good idea. Although some studies suggest that moderate alcohol use has health benefits, heavy or binge drinking over time can cause memory loss and permanent brain damage.
- Planning tasks, making "to do" lists, and using memory aids like notes and calendars can help you in dealing with forgetfulness. Some people find they remember things better if they mentally connect them to a familiar name, song, book, or TV show.

TIPS FOR COMMUNICATION WITH A PARENT WHO HAS MEMORY LOSS BEYOND THE NORM

Communication with a loved one who has Alzheimer's disease can be difficult and frustrating for the caregiver and the individual living with the disease. They may struggle with finding words, remembering what they want to say, understanding what words mean, and paying attention during conversations, and they may be sensitive to touch and to the tone and loudness of voices.

- Make eye contact and call your parent by name.
- Be aware of your tone, how loud your voice is, how you look at your parent, and your body language.
- Encourage two-way conversation for as long as possible.
- Use other methods besides speaking, such as gentle touching.
- Try distracting your parent if communication creates problems.
- Be patient with angry outbursts.
- Let your parent make some decisions and stay involved.
- Be open to their concerns, even if your parent is hard to understand.
- Behave in a warm, loving, and matter-of-fact manner.
- Hold your parent's hand while you talk.
- Use different words if your parent doesn't understand the first time. For example, if you ask your parent whether they are hungry and you don't get a response, you could say, "Dinner is ready now. Let's eat."
- Try not to say, "Don't you remember?" or "I told you."

Here are some tips for helping your parent when they know that they are having memory problems:[5]

- Take time to listen to your parent. They may want to talk about the changes they are noticing.
- Be sensitive and don't correct your parent every time they forget something or say something odd. Try to understand that it's a struggle for your parent to communicate.
- Help your parent try to find words to express thoughts and feelings. But be careful not to put words in the person's mouth or "fill in the blanks" too quickly.

Be aware of nonverbal communication. As people lose their ability to talk clearly, they may rely on other ways to communicate their thoughts and feelings.

Chapter Eleven

The Care and Maintenance of the Caregiver—*YOU*!

You are probably thinking, *Yeah, right! Who is going to care for me? There is too much to do and no time to do it!* I understand. My mom does not have anyone but me, so I work hard to be there for her during this time that she is caring for her own mother. Her mother takes advantage of her every way she possibly can—partly because this is her personality and partly because she is at a stage where she really can't help it and her judgment is not good. She doesn't realize she is running my mother into the ground both emotionally and physically. I remind my mother to set limits and boundaries. I also remind her that she is also a person with needs and feelings; her mother isn't the only one who does. My mother thanks me for my advice and heeds it for a few days, and then we have the same pep talk again.

As a caregiving daughter, you are most likely juggling responsibilities with work and/or raising adolescent children, or maybe you have adult children who have come back home to live. Maybe you are at an age where you are retired and have raised your children, but you would now like to be able to enjoy your grown children and grandchildren. Perhaps you would just like to be free to come and go as you please, with your spouse or significant other, or just be alone. Because you are juggling caregiving duties you are more likely to report sleep deprivation, poor eating habits, failure to exercise, failure to stay in bed when you are ill, fatigue, illness, and postponing of or failure to make medical appointments. Recently, my mother had a stomach bug and thought it best to stay clear of her mother so as not to pass it along, but she stayed away also because she was feeling so weak she couldn't even leave her house. Her mother became quite demanding, and she called her frequently and would yell into the phone that she needed help. My mother then contacted the paid caregiver (who goes over to provide care in the morning to my grandmother) to ask her to please hurry and go check to see if she was okay—that she had just called yelling for help. My mother soon received a call back from the paid care provider saying that everything was just fine. This was a manipulative "tactic" to get my mother to come running over to give my grandmother the attention she wanted. My mother couldn't even have peace of mind while she was sick and just rest because she was constantly being contacted by her mother. When she would answer the phone, her mother would say, "Are you still sick!?" and "When are you gonna get better!?" not "How are you?" Caregivers have often been referred to as "the other patient." I think this is quite fitting given all that they manage. Besides many of the physical reactions I mentioned, there are many emotional reactions to providing care, such as guilt, loss, anger, irritation, fear, worry, depression, embarrassment, helplessness, and isolation. There is a disruption in your needs and wants. You feel you need to forgo your plans, your dreams, or even just the opportunity to develop certain interests, enjoy "friend" time, have personal time, or take a vacation. All of this adds up to feeling like you have little control over your own life. My grandmother, at ninety-nine and a half, feels she has little control over her life, so she tries even harder to control my mother's life, thus exacerbating the strain my mother is already feeling.

CONCERNS FOR CAREGIVERS

There are a multitude of issues and concerns that create stress and strain for caregivers, which is why it is so critical that caregivers remember to take care of themselves. Some common concerns that caregivers have identified are listed here.

- Navigating the "system." Caregivers report having difficulty navigating the various kinds of care and supports that are available to older adults. One of the difficulties my mother has had is not with any specific kind of care (physical therapists, doctors, nurses, etc.). The problem has been with the questioning that she gets from health care professionals. She often feels interrogated. Each time she talks to a health care professional she gets the same questions: Is your mother alone? Who is caring for her? What is the schedule of care? You don't leave her alone, do you? One day, I heard my mother on the phone, and she finally said, "Do you folks have to ask me these same questions each time? Do you not document this somewhere? Do I have to be subjected to answering and telling her daily schedule each time I am contacted by you or when I contact you for a question?" She was just done and she was tired. I noticed that she is often treated as if she is not doing enough or questioned as if she is somehow lacking in the care she is providing. I told her it was good she clearly stated again the care her mother receives—morning, afternoon, and night. Perhaps each person who asked her these same series of questions felt they were just doing their job. But they were lacking sensitivity to the fact that my mother was exhausted, and being "questioned" when she needed support was simply not helpful. Perhaps questions asked in a different way could have helped the care professional understand what resources my mother already had in place and what she still may have needed. For example, "Does your mother need constant supervision?" "How much rest are you getting?" "Is there a service or resource that could be of help to you at this time?"

- Considerations of long-term care: Many caregivers, at some point in the caregiving process, find that they have to ask themselves the dreaded question of whether their loved one needs skilled care in an assisted living facility. The physical and cognitive functioning of your loved one, as well as the resources available, are some of the main considerations when making this determination.
- Finances: Financial tasks are often a part of providing care to aging parents. These can include writing checks, paying bills, providing financial support, helping manage resources, paying for essentials, and paying for luxuries.[1] Financial concerns are typically not the major source of concern for caregivers, but they can become so with increased inflation and continuing erosion of such aids as Social Security, pensions, and health insurance.[2] Inadequate financial resources cause additional stress for caregivers of a parent with dementia, since they may also be managing the household budget.

- Safety: This is a major concern for caregivers, particularly if they cannot be with their parent throughout the day. There are concerns surrounding slips and falls, burns and fires, and medication mix-ups that could lead to an overdose or poisoning.
- Time management: Performing daily tasks for a parent can often be very time consuming, especially as your parent becomes older and more dependent. The older caregivers become, so do their care-receivers, which means they are more frail and need more assistance. My mother, now 76, cares for her nearly 100-year-old mother. There are a number of women who are actually care-receivers at the age of 76—not the caregiver. The care my mother provides takes a toll on her mentally and physically. For women who are still working, they have to juggle the competing demands of an employer and often-times a spouse and children who are still living at home.
- Working full- or part-time: More than one in six Americans working full-time or part-time report assisting with the care of an aging or disabled family member or relative. On average, employed caregivers work 34.7 hours a week.[3] Some employers offer education and training, support, resources, and referral services to employees. Talk to your employer or Human Resources about policies, options, and what is available at your place of employment.
- Lack of respite (a rest from care): Respite can come in the form of formal services (paid support) or informal services (support from family and friends). As your loved one becomes more disabled and requires more care, formal supports are in order. Some families may move back and forth from formal to informal support depending on the changes in the care-receiver's functioning, or they may remain using one source regardless of the changes in the care-receiver, which can result in greater stress.[4] Unfortunately, family caregivers tend to "spend down" their physical and emotional resources before in-home services are utilized.[5]
- Physical strain: Physical health tends to decline in caregivers, as a result of sleep loss and the general physical demands that accompany caregiving duties. Caregivers often postpone attending to their own medical needs. Many caregivers suffer from physical distress known as "caregiver's syndrome"—the distress resulting from years of physical strain of lifting and turning a disabled adult. Other problems that can develop include bursitis, osteoporosis, and arthritis.[6] Physi-

cally ill caregivers, especially those with chronic progressive conditions, are more vulnerable and likely to need help.[7]

- Family conflict: Conflict within the family can erupt over such issues as disagreeing about how care is or should be provided, who should pay for what, division of your loved one's belongings when the time comes, and concerns about which family members are assisting and which ones are not.

- Functioning of your loved one: Older adults with decreased physical and/or cognitive functioning require more assistance from caregivers. This can result in a more negative impact on the household because it is a disruption in how the household functions, which in turn is more detrimental to the relationship between the caregiver and care-receiver.[8] Care-receiver behaviors that restrict or confine the caregiver have been linked to caregivers feeling burdened.[9] Caregivers also feel stress resulting from having to perform care tasks and activities, but these tasks and activities also create additional strain due to the infringement on the caregiver's time and energy.[10]

The first step in taking care of *you* is to recognize when you are feeling stressed. The literature on caregiving describes something called "subjective burden," which is the caregiver's emotional distress related to her situation and the extent to which she feels manipulated and oppressed by the demands of the care-receiver.[11] For some adult children, the very thought of caring for an older parent is overwhelming.[12] Sometimes there is a tendency to deny the actual situation. Adult children frequently have a persistent image of their parents as being strong, capable, and resistant to harm and illness. They "forget" that their parents are growing old and need assistance especially from their children. Once adult children realize this, the discrepancy between this idolized image of their parents and the reality of their parents' situation results in feelings of stress and anxiety.

The sudden need for ministry may also cause old conflicts and feelings to reappear. The relationship between parent and child is probably the deepest and most emotionally powerful of all human relationships, and the emotions produced in it are many. There is warmth and love, yet there are also negative emotions, feelings such as guilt and regret, anger, and frustration, which can hinder the relationship between parent and child.[13]

Regardless of the strength of the emotional tie linking the caregiver and care-receiver, some emotional stress is inevitable in caregiving. These stresses reflect practical frustrations in locating community programs, feeling socially isolated, anxiety that back-up services won't be available in times of crises, worry over your parent's health, and obtaining sufficient help. Caregivers experience difficulties reconciling the competing demands of child rearing and/or work with the care of their loved one. This can all result in feelings of exhaustion, discouragement, and isolation that seem relentless and overwhelming.[14]

SYMPTOMS OF EMOTIONALLY
BURDENED CAREGIVERS

Symptoms of emotionally burdened caregivers may be subtle enough to escape the notice of family or professionals but may be significant enough to interfere with the caregiver's ability to meet their obligations and changes that come with providing care to a loved one. Here are some emotional and physical reactions that caregivers can experience as a result of being overwhelmed by their situation.

Emotional Reactions

- Irritability
- Guilt
- Grief
- Loss
- Anger
- Worry
- Depression
- Embarrassment
- Helplessness
- Isolation
- Forgetfulness
- Anxiety
- Apathy and listlessness

Physical Reactions

- Fatigue
- Illness
- Poor eating habits
- Failure to exercise
- Failure to stay in bed when ill
- Physically handling your parent in a rough manner (hitting, pushing, shoving, yelling)

These emotional and physical reactions should be considered warning signs that you are showing signs of stress and possibly depression.

Here are some coping strategies to consider and try:

- Breathe: It sounds silly, but studies show that people under stress often forget to breathe. They only do shallow breathing. (When I play violin in public, my teacher actually has to write on my sheet music the word *breathe*. I get so stressed while playing that I will forget to breathe during an entire song!) Remember to deep breathe from your diaphragm. A diaphragmatic breathing technique is to place one hand on your upper chest and the other just below your rib cage. This will allow you to feel your diaphragm move as you breathe. Breathe in slowly through your nose so that your stomach moves out against your hand. The hand on your chest should remain as still as possible. Now, if this sounds too difficult, find a friend and have a glass of wine!
- Recognize your limitations: You can only do what you can do! Stop trying to do it all and be everything to everyone. Just say, "I've done what I can do and it's enough."
- Ask for help and say "yes" to it: My mother put an ad in our local paper for some morning help for my grandmother. There were a number of responses, particularly from women who really needed some extra money; some of them were retired, so their schedules were very accommodating. If you belong to a church, don't hesitate to see your church as a source of support. You could even reach out to the local high school's guidance counselor since they know of a number of high school students who are looking for after-school or summer jobs. A high school student could be a good source of support and would be great for doing yard work and repairs.

- Involve your family: Be sure to include your family in the family plan of doing things inside the house, helping with errands, or driving to appointments. Keep communication open and call a "family meeting" if you need to.
- Think about hiring a house cleaner: Have someone come to clean either your house or your parent's house every other week. If you live together, then you both end up with a clean house. Having a clean and organized home can really be a stress reliever.
- Stay in touch: Don't isolate yourself.
- Consider a support group: Chapter 13 gives information on a Facebook group for caregivers and a support line for caregivers. You can also join a local caregiver support group through your church or perhaps a referral from your health care professional. It can be very therapeutic to express your feelings in a group setting, listen to others' dilemmas, and ultimately do some creative problem solving together. Sometimes caregivers hesitate to attend a support group because it seems like just one more thing that takes up valuable time, especially if you are exhausted and you don't feel like being around a bunch of people you don't know. It is worth giving it a try, and one great option could be to try an online version of a support group.
- Consider spiritual resources: Don't forget about your local place of worship as a source of support. Being in a stressful situation can sometimes cause individuals to ask spiritual questions such as, "Why did God put me in this situation?" "Why do I have to suffer through this?" "Will God forgive me if I can't always do this with love?"
- Make a routine: A daily caregiving schedule that everyone is familiar with and can count on is essential. That way your parent and anyone else involved in the care knows what to expect. My mother, for example, has a paid care provider go to my grandmother's home for three hours in the morning (by the way, my grandmother still lives with her husband, so she is not alone). The expectation is that the care provider will straighten things up in the main living area, get breakfast, change my grandmother's adult diaper, and give morning medications. Then when my mother arrives for her shift, she has her set of care tasks and activities to perform. This way my grandmother knows what to expect and when. It keeps the day running fairly smoothly except for the occasional difficult behaviors of refusing to eat or having her adult diaper changed—again, this is for another chapter!

- Eat well: Nutrient dense foods are so important!
- Get much needed and deserved rest: Find a quiet place to nap, take a bath, read a book, sit outside and watch the sunset—anything that you can do to just have some time for you to take a quiet break or just get some sleep.
- Brisk walking: If you hate exercise, then walking is a wonderful way to break up stress, to get out of the house, and to get moving. If you don't want to walk briskly, then just walk—peacefully.
- Do something that has nothing to do with caregiving! You need to have somewhere to go to get away. Go get a cup of coffee/tea, stroll the mall, get a mani-pedi, take a class, meet a friend, drive, or walk—anything to get away for a while. Remember: love yourself. You matter!
- Lean on your friends for a listening ear or a cup of tea or glass of wine.
- Recognize when a change is needed: Create a space just for yourself either indoors or outdoors. Find someone who understands what you are going through.
- Keep your self-talk positive: It is easy to lapse into negative self-talk when we are under stress. Remind yourself that you are doing the best you can! Don't forget that the work you are doing is significant and that you should feel proud of your efforts.
- Learn to forgive others and allow yourself to experience gratitude.
- Understand that you do not have to do it all: Be sure to get some scheduled relief from others, so that you have something to look forward to.
- Begin to keep a journal: There are an abundance of journals you can find online or at the bookstore. Look for one that you feel will meet your needs. For example, perhaps you just want a journal that is blank and then each day you write down your own thoughts and feelings that maybe start with something like "Today, I feel . . ." or "Today, I am worried about . . ." You might want a journal that gives you writing prompts for each day, and there are lots of those out there. If you don't like to write, please don't think that a journal pins you down to writing a lot. Maybe each day, or every other day, you just write a sentence or two or even just a thought you are having. I found a pack of very pretty journals that includes a six-pack of dual-tip markers and four petite planners: a budget book, a wellness log,

a self-care journal, and a gratitude journal. You can find this pack at www.qvc.com (H224347; Erin Condren Wellness & Self-Care Journal Bundle). Journaling can help you be mindful of emotions you didn't even know you were feeling, and it can even help you work through those feelings without fear of judgment. If you need something that tracks the care of your parent and you have a paid care provider coming into your home, then I found one by Jason Soft (2018) called Personal Caregiver Log Book. Any pen and paper will do, but these are just some suggestions if you need some help to get started.

And finally, let go of these misconceptions:

- "I am responsible for my parent's health." I have told my mother many times that her mother is responsible for where she is with her health at this point in time. Her mother made choices that led to her decline in physical mobility. She refuses to do her physical therapy, she refuses to get up and move, she refuses to drink enough fluids, she often refuses to eat (her mother does not have dementia, so these are the choices she makes). I remind my mother that she can offer food and fluids regularly, that she can suggest that her mother come and sit at the table so that she can get moving a little bit, and that her mother can have the physical therapist come to the house. But ultimately, my grandmother is responsible for the decisions she makes, and my mother can't force her to do anything and cannot take on the responsibility of feeling the guilt when she sees declines in her mother's physical mobility.
- "If I don't do it, no one will." This statement goes back to the suggestion of getting other people on board to assist so that you are not doing it all.
- "If I do it right, I will get the love, attention, and respect I deserve." My mother is still living under this misconception and has for years, and she is still not getting the love and respect she deserves. In fact, she is getting less of these things as the years go by. My grandmother and her husband, at times, treat my mother with disrespect, and she is only as good as the last thing she did for them. It is very sad to see that her years of devotion and love did not seem to matter or count for anything.

Chapter Twelve

Dealing with Difficult Behaviors

My mother sometimes feels like she is going to lose her mind after she has been with her mother for hours providing care. It isn't the actual care tasks that drive her crazy. She is happy to prepare meals for her mother, get medications organized, do her laundry, straighten the house, brush her hair, or change any bandages from small abrasions. What just about pushes my mother over the edge are the controlling or manipulative behaviors my grandmother exhibits. For example, she has been refusing to have my mother change her pull-up diapers, freshen her up with cleansing wipes, give her a sponge bath, and then get her changed into fresh lounge wear. She will say, "I will tell you when I want those things done!" But, then of course the day will pass and she doesn't want those things done. She has been refusing to eat her morning Cream of Wheat cereal and, after a bite, will purposefully let it dribble out of her mouth and say, "I don't want it!" My grandmother used to really enjoy going out to the mailbox each day to get the mail. That was something that was very important to her. She used to always handle the business end of the farm and all the bills. She had a fabulous head for math and accounting, and so getting the mail was part of keeping track of what was coming in and what was going on. Her husband gets the mail now because she isn't able to, and so when he isn't around, she gets up with her walker and gets the mail off the table and hides it in her bed. My mother will pull back the covers to help my grandmother sit up to eat, only to discover a pile of mail that she has been hoarding. It is her one last attempt to "hold on" to some sense of control. That is often what many of these difficult behaviors are about—the desire to simply have control. She has lost so much of the control over the life she used to have, and she wants to regain it. My grandmother would never want to not be clean and fresh, but if it means to have some say about her daily life, then she will sit in wet pull-ups and unclean pajamas. Sometimes behaviors that are out of character are, of course, related to dementia, and that is simply not in anyone's control. There are some wonderful books and websites on the subject of dealing with behaviors when you are caring for someone with dementia. What do you do when it is just your parent being difficult (for whatever reasons)? Sometimes it is just about being creative, and many of you reading this could probably write your own chapter on this very subject and what you have tried and what works for you and what doesn't work. Some of the suggestions for dealing with difficult behaviors come from AgingCare.com,[1] and others are just related to personal experiences.

STRATEGIES FOR DEALING WITH DIFFICULT BEHAVIORS

First, here are some suggestions for situations when your parent is being difficult and you don't know what they want or need and you are getting more frustrated by the minute:

Frustration (Both You and Your Parent)

Try sitting calmly and asking one or more of these questions:

- How can I help?
- What do you need from me?
- Is there anything I can do?

Or try one of these:

- Mother, here is a pen and paper. Write down some things I can do for you today.
- Do you want to make a list of some things you would like for me to do for you?

Meals or Drinking Enough Fluids

My grandmother was becoming overwhelmed at mealtime, seeing a big lunch meat sandwich put in front of her. Afterall, she cannot hold onto the sandwich very well, and her teeth and chewing are really declining. She also has been getting distracted by having to come and sit at the kitchen table. Her husband keeps *everything* on the kitchen table—so the table is just a clutter zone. My grandmother, who was once a neat freak, is completely overwhelmed by the messy table. My mother tries to straighten it daily, but he scolds her and tells her not to move anything because he knows where everything is on that table! So, as you can imagine, mealtime has been disastrous with the messy table and my grandmother not being able to hold onto food or chew very well. Here is what we came up with:

• Situating her sitting up on the couch wearing a large bib with a tray on her lap (she loves it!)
• Putting small pieces of lunch meat, cheese cubes, fruit, nuts/raisins, crackers, cottage cheese, potato salad, and a cookie into a small, compartmentalized tray. This way, it is manageable to touch, hold, and eat. She uses a plastic fork, which is lighter weight, and she drinks a juice pouch or juice box because it is much easier for her to hold and she doesn't have to tip it up. She loves drinking out of a straw and will actually finish all of her liquid. She has been doing so much better eating and drinking with this new method. As for the morning Cream of Wheat, I told my mother, "Stop giving it to her. Instead try a poached egg in a dish with toast cut up into small pieces." This is now a favorite. By the way, the compartmentalized tray offers choices, and she likes to look at the tray and choose what to eat first or next.

Changing Clothes/Diapering/Bathing

You might have to lower your standards as to what you think is cleanliness. Bathing once or twice a week is typically enough to avoid skin infections. Perhaps start with asking if you can wash their face and then continue with wiping down other parts and explaining what you are doing as you go. There are any number of reasons for a parent refusing to change clothes or be bathed—fear of falling, modesty, pain, depression, and not realizing how long it has been since they were last cleaned and changed. And of course, dementia can also be the issue. Here are some things to consider:

- Try having someone else do the bathing, like a paid care provider. This sometimes works.
- Have your parent's doctor talk with them about the importance of hygiene. Older adults often feel that their doctor "knows best."
- Reward your parent by saying, "If we get all cleaned up, how about . . ." and then offer whatever might be a positive reward for them, such as having a visitor or going out to a favorite restaurant.
- Talk about getting cleaned up like it is "spa day." Purchase some new bath products, nice smelling lotion, and maybe some new pajamas or nightgown. Try purchasing a new brand of pull-up/diaper and say, "Let's try these!"

Rage/Anger/Yelling/Crying

My grandmother is often very angry, and she yells and cries when she sees my mother. She isn't yelling at my mother; she's just yelling and crying about her situation. She is angry at her husband, but they have always had a tumultuous relationship of arguing and each trying to control the other and each trying to "win." They are no different at ninety and ninety-nine years of age. Kind of sad, really. His declining health has caused him to be particularly unkind and impatient. My mother has tried to get her mother to come and live with her or to go to an assisted living facility, but my grandmother says that she is not leaving her house and that he should be the one to leave. The argumentative nature of both my grandmother and her husband has always been part of their relationship, but now it has intensified.

Mental and physical frustrations come with aging, but they intensify any negative personality tendencies that were already present. Please note that it is important to first rule out anything that might be causing a personality change such as a urinary tract infection (UTI) or dehydration; even certain medication combinations or medication toxicity can cause a change in personality. Some medications can have a negative effect on personality such as blood pressure medications and anti-inflammatories, so be sure to check with your parent's doctor. Pain and boredom can also create a breeding ground for negative personality traits to bubble over. Personality changes that are creating havoc for everyone should be explored with your parent's doctor. Sometimes an anti-anxiety or anti-psychotic medication or an antidepressant is needed. If it is dementia, there are medications to help minimize the personality changes.

Here are some things to try:

• Try to focus on the positive
• Let them vent
• Try an activity together, after they have let off some steam

Paranoia/Hallucinations

My grandmother does not hear well at all—even with her hearing aids—and she is convinced that when her husband is talking with someone else that they are plotting against her. She becomes terribly upset and cries. Again, she does not have dementia, but her poor vision coupled with her severe hearing loss, added to a verbally abusive relationship with her husband adds up to her belief that he is plotting her demise. My mother will simply say something like, "Mother, what he was saying was . . ." She just gives factual information. Sometimes paranoia and hallucinations are a side effect of a medication or a UTI.

• The best thing you can do is to simply validate, comfort, and try to reassure that everything is okay. Do not try to convince your parent that they are wrong. This will only serve to agitate them further. When I say *validate*, I mean you should simply say, "I understand" and provide empathy. What they are seeing, hearing, and thinking is very real to them. Also, giving some factual information could be helpful, but disagreeing or arguing with them is not.
• Don't argue.
• Try not to react if they blame you for something.
• Let the person know that they are safe.
• Use gentle touching or hugging to show you care.
• Search for things to distract your parent, then talk about what you found, for example, a photograph or keepsake.

Strange Obsessions

Saving tissues, constantly picking at their skin, hypochondria, and worrying over dates/times are all types of obsessive behaviors. Obsessive behavior can be related to anxiety, depression, dementia, and other neurological issues. These behaviors should be discussed with your parent's doctor because sometimes therapy and/or medication is needed. Here are some tips:

* The most important thing is to watch for triggers—things that make the behavior worse. If it is related to a specific event or activity, then avoid whatever that is as much as possible.
* Do not participate in their obsession or encourage it in any way.
* Distract and redirect.
* Try to eliminate the trigger of the obsession. For example, with skin picking, try to keep the skin moisturized and covered to help minimize the picking and itching.

Hoarding

This is really a tough one because it could be the onset of a form of dementia or a pre-Alzheimer's issue. If it is extreme hoarding, then medication and counseling can make a big difference. Oftentimes the hoarding occurs because they cannot decide what to do with items, and they can no longer make decisions about how to organize. Your parent may also talk about how important the items are to them, and they fear their memories will be lost. Here are some ideas:

* Offering to help sort, give away, or throw away items could help.
* Start small—maybe one area, one table, one room, or one cabinet (have them help you, of course, so that you are not doing it without their permission).
* Make a memory box for some things that seem particularly special.
* If the hoarding is an issue to health and safety, then you will need the help of adult protective services if your parent cannot or will not address the hoarding problem.
* Sometimes the home is just an unclean, disorganized mess, but health and safety are not an issue. It might be that your standards have to be adjusted. My grandmother's home used to be absolute perfection.

It was a show-stopper, one of a kind, beautiful home. Now, it smells when you walk in and there is just so much clutter everywhere, but it is not a health and safety hazard.

Refusing to Allow an Outside Care Provider to Come to the Home

Some of the reasons for this could be fear of strangers, resentment of thinking that their family does not want to provide care, or embarrassment about how the house looks or that they need someone to help. For example, my grandmother is too embarrassed to have someone come in to clean her home. She says, "It's too dirty. I don't want anyone to see it." Here are some suggestions:

- Have your parent "interview" two or three paid care providers and let them choose the person that they think they would feel most comfortable having in the house doing the various tasks they need done. If it is their idea, then it is the best idea.
- Suggest that they just try having someone come once a week and "see how it goes." Start with some simple kinds of things for the care provider to do, like vacuuming or making a light lunch.

Demanding Undivided Attention

Setting boundaries with a demanding parent is critical, and failing to do so can result in frustration and burnout. Here are some things to consider:

- It's hard and takes practice, but you have to give up the notion that you can control a dysfunctional or toxic person's behavior. When you give up on this notion, you stop allowing them to control your emotions and behaviors. When your parent sees that they cannot get the reactions out of you that they used to by pushing your buttons, then they are left to deal with the consequences of their behaviors and decisions. That is what you need to understand. It is about their behaviors and their decisions—not something that you did or didn't do.
- You can let them know you love them but that you will not tolerate being manipulated with fear, obligation, or guilt. Choose not to

participate in problems that are not yours. Self-preservation is the key. Otherwise, you will end up being so burned-out and emotionally fragile that you won't be able to care for your parent—or you might even turn abusive yourself, which has happened to some caregivers.

• Try to get them involved in outside activities. If they are housebound, then get others involved in coming to the home to provide some companionship, even if it is paid help/assistance.

Overspending or Extreme Frugality

When an older adult loses independence, they often try to make up for it by doing things like overspending or saving to an extreme. It can be very embarrassing, for you and your parent, bringing up the subject of money when funds are being mismanaged. Perhaps bringing in a third party such as a spiritual leader or financial advisor is one way to get the conversation going, and it needs to be with someone your parent trusts. Keep in mind that not being able to handle their money is one of the early signs of dementia, or perhaps they have always been poor at handling their funds and now it has become a real problem. If it seems that your parent cannot understand the seriousness of the situation, it might be best for you to put a stop to some of the things that you might be able to control, such as clubs and memberships that keep sending them things in exchange for their money. Also, if creditors keep calling, then you can work out a payment plan to try to get finances back on track. If the other extreme is a problem, whereby you are doing all the spending because they simply are being too frugal, then show them a list of all of your expenses for their care—it may help your parent come to realize that they don't want to burden you financially.

In reading this chapter, you may have thought to yourself, *My parent has more than just one of these difficult behaviors*. My mother noticed that her mother had four of these behaviors and said, "No wonder I feel overwhelmed!" She also commented that her mother's husband has two of the difficult behaviors (hoarding and overspending—different ones than the ones her mother has). Hopefully, you can find a helpful hint or two in this chapter that may just do the trick in either alleviating the problem or at least lessening it a bit.

Concerns about Abuse and Safety

Maybe you are caring for a parent who is verbally abusive or you are caring for your parent where someone else in the home is abusive. The best thing to do in this situation is to get as much outside assistance as you can, such as a paid care provider, and enlist the help of social services—and, if necessary, law enforcement, depending on the severity of the situation and how unsafe you may feel. While my mother was providing care to her mother, verbal abuse from another family member was daily, and threats of physical violence from yet another family member became part of her caregiving reality. She was navigating a situation of concern for her mother's well-being and concern for her own safety. She tried to get her mother to come live with her, but her mother did not want to leave her own home; she learned from social services that you cannot remove someone from their home against their will. No doubt, it was terrible circumstances under which she had to provide care to her mother.

Chapter Thirteen

Navigating the System

Parent care involves a constant tension between attachment and loss, pleasing and caring, seeking to preserve an older person's dignity and exerting unaccustomed authority, overcoming resistance to care and fulfilling extravagant demands, reviving a relationship and transforming it.

—Steven Abel[1]

First of all, what kind of system are you navigating? Is it the health care system or the "sick care" system? Which seems to be the more appropriate title? Is it a system or a maze? We all hope to get care for our loved ones that feels caring and feels seamless as we progress through whatever process is needed to get us back to some sense of normalcy. Unfortunately, when something happens—a fall, a stroke, a heart attack, or worsening signs of dementia, for example—we are now making decisions while in crisis mode.

Each time something happens to my grandmother—which is always a fall that puts her in the hospital and then into an assisted living facility for the allotted period of time to receive physical therapy to "get back on her feet"—my mother always feels as though she is starting over. With each fall, there is a different set of problems to navigate. Sometimes it is a fracture; the most recent fall resulted in a concussion and a brain bleed that had to be monitored. The doctor strongly encouraged my mother, once my grandmother was discharged, to have her go to an assisted living facility, where she could be monitored 24/7 and receive physical therapy to gain back some strength. My mother was torn for two days with what she should do because this was during the COVID-19 pandemic, and pandemic-related restrictions would prevent her from visiting her mother daily. Under normal circumstances, she would be able to visit her, and this would keep her mother happy during the three weeks she would stay at the assisted living facility. My mother could monitor care, ask questions, and tend to additional care needs while she was there, which the staff always appreciated. My mother made the decision in the best interests of her mother's health and safety to send her to assisted living. She paid a high price for that decision. Her mother called her, literally, "round the clock." She had a phone in her room and called her continuously during the day and all through the night, and each call was not a conversation. Her mother would cry and yell into the phone, "Come and get me! How could you do this to me? Where are you? I wouldn't do this to you!" My mother was so exhausted from these calls that she finally requested that they remove the phone from her mother's room, but they told her that legally they could not do this. Each day, we would deliver handwritten cards and notes of love, along with treats and magazines, but she wanted nothing to do with any of that. She wanted to come home, and my mother suffered from guilt, confusion, and exhaustion because the doctor insisted her mother was where she needed to be in order to recover properly. It was a nightmare. I completely empathize with all the families and the older adults who felt separated, cut off from each other, and alone during the pandemic. Not seeing your loved one—because you love them and don't want to risk them getting sick and you want them to be safe—feels all wrong, especially when you know they are hurting and alone.

GETTING INFORMATION AND FINDING SERVICES

To start, I would recommend a wonderful service called Eldercare Locator. It is the first step to finding resources for older adults in any US community. It is a free national information and referral service of the Administration on Aging that provides an instant connection to resources that can help your parent have a little more independence and offers support for you. Their toll free number is 1-800-677-1116. They also have a website (eldercare.acl.gov) to help you find essential resources. The website includes things like a "Caregiver Corner" with answers to the most frequently asked questions that their call center receives from caregivers; a "Learn More About" section that provides information on popular topics like transportation, support services, housing, health, insurance, and benefits; and brochures on topics important to health and well-being. You can also find out information about whether your state offers pay for family caregivers, find free or low-cost legal assistance, find a State Health Insurance Counseling Program, find out how to launch a complaint against a long-term care facility, and get many other kinds of questions answered related to caregiving.

Resources

- American Association of Retired Persons (AARP; www.aarp.org).
- Caregiver Support Line (1-877-333-5885).
- Facebook Group for Caregivers: Caring for Elderly Parents and Helping Them Age with Dignity. Facebook.com.
- National Institute on Aging (NIA; www.nia.nih.gov): Provides guides and fact sheets.
- Family Caregiver Alliance (www.caregiver.org): Information on programs.
- Caring.com: Information, support, in-home care, and senior living options.
- National Alliance for Caregiving (www.caregiving.org): Provides information on resources and programs.
- National Family Caregiver Support Program (https://acl.gov/pro grams/support-caregivers/national-family-caregiver-support -program): Funds a variety of supports that help family and informal caregivers care for older adults in their homes for as long as possible.
- Healthfinder.gov: Health and wellness topics.
- Helpguide.org: Their mission is to help people overcome mental and emotional health issues and live fuller, happier lives.
- Caregiver Action Network (CAN; caregiveraction.org): Education, peer support, and resources.
- Alzheimer's Association (alz.org): Information on the disease, dementia symptoms, diagnosis, stages, treatment, and care and support resources.

- AgingCare (Agingcare.com): Caregiver support, elder care resources, senior housing, in-home care.
- National Respite Locater (ARCH; https://archrespite.org/respiteloca tor): Helps find respite services in your area that meet your needs.
- Health Resources and Services Administration (HRSA; bhw.hrsa .gov): Offers training curriculum modules for workers and caregivers.
- Veterans Association Caregiver Support Line (1-855-260-3274 or www.caregiver.va.gov): Provides resources for caregivers of veterans.
- State Health Insurance Assistance Program (SHIPS; www.shiptacen ter.org): Offers no-cost, unbiased health benefit counseling, education, and advocacy services to help people make informed benefit choices.
- Partnership for Prescription Assistance (www.pparx.org): Provides a list of patient assistance programs supported by pharmaceutical companies.
- National Domestic Violence Hotline 1-800-799-7233.
- Aging Disability Resource Center (ADRC): Information, advice, counseling, options, services, and supports. Contact information for an ADRC near you can be found through the Eldercare Locator.
- National Council on Aging (NCOA): Partners with nonprofit organizations, government, and businesses to provide innovative community programs and services, online help, and advocacy. By providing some general information about your parent, you can see a list of possible benefits you might want to explore (www.benefitscheckup.org).
- Medicaid (www.medicaid.gov): People on fixed incomes who have limited resources may qualify for Medicaid. This program covers the costs of medical care for people of all ages who have limited income and meet other eligibility requirements.
- Program for All-Inclusive Care for the Elderly (PACE; www.pace 4you.org): Under Medicare, some states have PACE. This program provides care and services to people who otherwise would need care in a nursing home.
- Falls Prevention Resource Center through the National Council on Aging (ncoa.org): Provides a falls prevention conversation guide for caregivers. Resources include educational brochures, tip sheets, videos, blogs, exercise and physical activity guidebooks, motivational flyers, and success stories.

- Hospice Care (Caring.com): This site can find hospice care options near you. Hospice services offer physical, emotional, spiritual, and practical comfort and support to patients and families who are facing death—at home, in the hospital, or in other settings.
- Long-Term Care Ombudsman (acl.gov): You can locate your state's LTC Ombudsman at this site. An LTC Ombudsman works to resolve problems related to health, safety, welfare, and rights of individuals who live in long-term care facilities.

In-Home and Community Services

You have heard the oft-repeated saying, "All it takes is money!" Well, unfortunately, that is true even in the world of caring for your aging parents. Paid care and support is provided typically based on the aging individual's or couple's income and/or assets. A majority of older adults cannot afford paid home care. If they can, they cannot afford care for a sustained period of time because it often involves substantial out-of-pocket expenses.

A 2019 article about the financial burden of paid home care disclosed that the national median hourly rate for home health aide services in 2018 was $22, only 11 percent of adults ages sixty-five and older were covered by private long-term care insurance in 2014, Medicare does not generally cover nonmedical home care services, and Medicaid finances home care only for people with very limited financial resources. Home care is less affordable for those who most need it, particularly those who are eighty-five and over and those who most likely need long-term care.[2] Here are some examples of paid home health care:

Case management: This is a service provided by a health care or social service provider. They will assess, plan, locate, and coordinate services for your loved one.

Homemakers and home health aides: These are trained professionals who provide assistance with grocery shopping, light housekeeping, meal preparation, and laundry. Aides also provide assistance with bathing, dressing, walking, and giving oral medications.

Physical therapists: These professionals will help improve movement and manage pain. They also can teach caregivers techniques for assisting with exercises and mobility.

Occupational therapists: They will teach skills for activities of daily living to help promote independence.

Social workers: They help people solve and cope with problems in their everyday lives. They can help caregivers find services, handle conflict among families, and assist with crisis situations.

Speech therapists: They facilitate the recovery from problems with speaking and swallowing.

Nutritionists: A nutritionist reviews dietary habits and makes recommendations for improvements. They can also help with information about special diet requirements.

In-home meal delivery: A hot meal is delivered at lunchtime for a fee. Some meal programs will also deliver a meal for the evening as well, and you can also order frozen meals to be put in the freezer and used when needed.

Adult day care: This service provides structured weekday programs of recreational activities, health services, and rehabilitation services to older adults.

Emergency Response System: These are devices worn by the older person that allows the older person to summon, by voice or signal, a trained worker at an emergency center.

Senior centers: These centers offer a variety of social, health, nutritional, educational, and recreational services.

Transportation: Contact your local Area Agency on Aging to find out more about local senior transportation. Many counties have Dial-A-Ride phone numbers to call for transportation.

Respite services: These services offer a few hours to several days of relief for caregivers. Contact your local Area Agency on Aging to find out more about respite services in your area.

Information and referral: This is provided at no cost by your local Area Agency on Aging. You can first start with Eldercare Locator as suggested earlier in this chapter.

Red Cross: Your local American Red Cross can also be a great source of information and support.

END-OF-LIFE CHOICES

Part of navigating the system is knowing what to do when there are end-of-life decisions to be made. Hopefully, you know your loved one's wishes, but many adult children and parents are uncomfortable having this conversation, and, therefore, end-of-life wishes and choices are not known until it is a crisis situation. Your parent may have expressed the wish to die at home; however, when the time comes, there may be issues that surround that choice, such as the fact that, even though you might have hospice services, most of the care falls on the family, and hospice is typically for those with six months to one year to live. When families do decide to go to the hospital, unless they have very clear written directives in place about their medical choices, then their care decisions are made by the health care professionals whose job is to promote life. The best thing to do to eliminate any confusion about end-of life choices is to have up-to-date documents in place, so everybody is aware of what to expect. One way to have this conversation is to say, "Mom, it would be so much easier for me to understand what you want so I can carry out your wishes. If something happened to you, it would be really hard for me to make those decisions. Maybe we can talk about it. I have some papers that might make it easier for us to work through." These documents can be put together by an attorney, or you can go to AARP .com and choose your state, then download your free advance directives. You will also find instructions for how to fill out the forms. End-of-life choice forms can include the following:

Advance Directive: This is a written statement of a person's wishes regarding medical treatment, often including a living will, made to ensure those wishes are carried out should the person be unable to communicate them to the doctor.

Living Will: This is a written statement detailing a person's desires regarding their medical treatment in circumstances in which they are no longer able to express informed consent.

Durable Power of Attorney for Health Care: A person designates an agent to make all decisions related to their health care in the event they become unable to make those decisions.

Durable Power of Attorney for Property: A person designates an agent to make financial decisions for them in the event they become unable to make those decisions.

Here is a list of other kinds of information you might want to collect and keep updated:[3]

- Birth certificate
- Social Security and Medicare numbers

- Education and military records
- Sources of income and assets
- Insurance policies, bank accounts, deeds
- Most recent tax return
- Credit card account names and numbers
- Safe deposit box key and information

PROVIDING CARE DURING A GLOBAL PANDEMIC

As if being a caregiver to your aging parent wasn't already challenging in terms of decision making, the COVID-19 pandemic now has created a whole other set of challenges for caregivers to face.[4] Several people suggested I write about the pandemic and how it has affected caregivers and their loved ones. I also had several people say that perhaps I should not write about it because it would "date" my book. Clearly, I chose to add it because COVID-19 has not been the first global virus, nor will it be the last, and families will have to learn to navigate how to care for frail, aging parents in this new world.

According to the US Bureau of Labor Statistics, roughly 40 million Americans were providing unpaid care to aging family members before the COVID-19 pandemic.[5] The number could be higher now given that caregivers are having to bring their parents home from assisted living facilities, where the virus has caused fatalities. Caregivers who once relied on adult day care and/or home health services are now having to discontinue those services in order to minimize contact with the outside world for parents whose immune systems are already compromised. It can be particularly challenging caring for someone with Alzheimer's disease or other dementia because they might be having a hard time navigating all the changes they are seeing around them.

If your parent doesn't already live with you, but you are considering bringing them to your home, make sure your home is safe with regard to mobility issues. Sometimes Area Agencies on Aging can do in-home assessments to help determine what is needed. The Families First Coronavirus Response Act allocated money for Older American Act nutrition programs, so that local agencies can provide meals to older adults.

Some Helpful Tips

- Order groceries online and have them delivered to your parent's home (if your parent does not live with you) or to your home if your parent lives with you. This helps minimize the contact that you have with outside places.
- If and when possible, consider having your parent's doctor's appointments online—either by phone or video chat.
- If you do decide to cut back on how many home health workers are coming to your home, consider how important physical therapy is to your parent. It may be the difference between being able to stay home or being admitted to the hospital. Remember that home health workers are required to follow the Centers for Disease Control Guidelines.
- Keep a thirty-day supply of all the medications and personal care supplies your parent needs. You should remember to do this for yourself as well, so that you stay on track and healthy.
- Keep a well-stocked food pantry.
- Practice frequent hand-washing.
- Wear a face mask when in public.
- Use hand sanitizer after each place you stop if you have been out running errands.
- If you do get sick, make sure you have a plan in place. Identify people who are your back-up caregivers and who can step in if needed.
- AARP has weekly webcasts about COVID-19 and what it means for older adults and their caregivers.

These tips will help keep you not only prepared but also hopefully healthy and safe and will minimize the risk of you spreading the virus to your loved ones.

Family members who either have their parent in an assisted living facility or have to place them in a facility during the pandemic are faced with not being able to visit their loved one. The options for this are few. Of course, they can always be contacted by phone, but oftentimes issues with hearing impairments cause frustration for both you and your aging parent. Another option and one that may or may not work, depending on the facility, is seeing/visiting your parent through a window. This may have worked for some, and that is wonderful; however, sometimes there are challenges that go along with this idea, for example, not being able to get to the window—maybe it is not accessible because of a hill, bushes, flowers, or the window is too high. Perhaps your loved one can't get to the window and special arrangements have to be made to have someone bring them to the window with the aid of a wheelchair or walker. Because they can't hear you and can only see you, they may be confused about why they are seeing you outside the window, especially if they have dementia or other cognitive impairment. They also may become emotional about seeing you because they cannot be with you. My grandmother had to go to an assisted living facility for about seven days after a fall; her bedroom window was not accessible, and she could not hear my mother's voice over the phone. The only way they could communicate was through a prearranged time. My mother had to call when a nurse was in the room, and then the nurse would relay messages back and forth between the two. My grandmother was furious about this situation, and she let us know it, too, on the day we picked her up!

For those who cannot visit by phone or waving through the window, a great option is to drop off cards, letters, treats, snacks, photos, a favorite sweater, a blanket, lotion, or other things similar that provide comfort and let your parent know that you love them and have not forgotten about them. There is no easy solution or one best answer. Families are doing their best to be creative during these times, so that their loved ones don't feel alone. You just have to do the best you can with what works for you and your family, taking in all considerations and weighing all the risks and options. It's really all any of us can do in these confusing times.

COVID-19 Resources

- Coronavirus.gov is the source for the latest information about COVID-19 prevention, symptoms, and answers to common questions.
- CDC.gov/coronavirus has the latest public health and safety information from the Centers for Disease Control and for the overarching medical and health provider community on COVID-19.
- USA.gov has the latest information about what the US government is doing in response to COVID-19.
- Medicare.gov has Medicare and coronavirus information.

Chapter Fourteen

Life after Caregiving: Now What?

I was telling my mother that I was going to write this chapter about losing your parent. She said, "My mother is still alive, but I have already lost her. I am not caring for the mother that I remember." I had not thought about loss in this way: she feels a tremendous sense of loss even before her mother has died. I am familiar with families who are caring for a loved one with dementia describing this feeling of loss for the person they once knew, but there is still that sense of loss for caregivers who remember their parent as vital, interactive, and capable, and they now must reconcile that with what they currently see and deal with on a daily basis. My mother is already mourning the loss of her best friend, even though her mother is still physically present. In many ways, I am realizing this loss for caregiving daughters is just as painful. Each day there is hope that maybe they can get back a little of what they feel is lost and it just doesn't materialize, and then there is disappointment—perhaps it is from dementia or maybe it is from age-related physical and cognitive decline. I wanted to acknowledge that is a very real loss. When you are a caregiver, you can experience feelings of loss before, during, and after the caregiving process. Dementia and chronic illness do bring about dramatic changes in our loved ones, and consequently there is a sense of loss in those of us who see these changes.

Eventually, you will face the physical loss of your parent—the one you are currently caring for. You may recall a much earlier chapter regarding the caregiving daughters who were either no longer caring for their mothers because their mothers were in long-term care or had died. They all had similar thoughts about this transition to no longer being caregivers:

* They would not go back and change anything.
* They did the best they could.
* They had no regrets.
* They felt they had no choice.
* They felt they did what they had to do.
* They had more positive perceptions of the situation than they had reported at the time of the first interview
* They felt a sense of relief.
* They felt a sense of loneliness and loss: What should I do with my time?

I hope, in reading some of these main thoughts that were shared by the caregiving daughters, that when the time comes, you can find some hope that you, too, will feel that you have no regrets and that you did the best you could. Of course, there will be a sense of loss and loneliness and feelings of grief, so I have included in this chapter some important information about the kinds of things you may go through and how to best deal with your emotions.

Some important considerations as you move into this next phase of your life (whenever that may be—remember, this chapter is here as a resource for you whether that is five months, five years, or fifteen years from now):

* Allow time for grief: Don't bury your emotions or tell yourself that you need to just "get over" it.
* Expect some loneliness: After all, you have been caring for your parent every day, and they have been a part of your life always. Of course, you are going to feel lonely.
* Forgive: If you had any relationship issues with your parent or others involved in the family, it is best to just let go of these issues—for your own mental and physical well-being. It is time to just put those things to rest.
* Remember the good times: If times were hard during caregiving, then it might take some time to recall the good times, but once you allow yourself to grieve and let go of the stress you may have been under, you will begin to remember the good.

• Accept your feelings: Don't be hard on yourself or judge yourself. Just meet yourself where you are with your feelings and just have those feelings. Use your journal, if you started one, to help you work through some of those feelings.

GRIEF

Allow Yourself Time to Grieve

• Allow quiet time alone to think
• Be open to your feelings
• Tell your story
• Say good-bye
• Allow yourself to cry
• Share your memories

In adjusting to your loss, don't be afraid if you notice some physical and mental changes and/or reactions. These are normal responses to grief and loss, so be patient with yourself if you notice these changes:

• Upset stomach
• Shortness of breath
• Heart palpitations
• Tightness in the throat and dizziness
• Trouble sleeping
• Little interest in food
• Loss of energy
• Trouble with concentration
• A hard time making decisions

There are other things you might experience:

• Helplessness
• Sleeplessness
• Emptiness
• Depression
• Worry/confusion
• Loss of control

- Anxiety and fear
- Isolation

In addition to dealing with feelings of loss, you also may need to put your own life back together. Perhaps there was only time to focus on the care of your parent, and now you have to refocus your time. This can be hard, and it takes patience with yourself to, perhaps, relearn how to spend your time. Some people feel better sooner than they expect. Others may take longer.

Be sure to take care of yourself while you are grieving. In the beginning, you are busy with details and family and friends who are around you to assist and visit, but then things slow down and you feel the changes. Here are some ideas to keep in mind:

- Take care of yourself: Grief can be hard on your health. Exercise regularly, eat healthy food, and get enough sleep. Bad habits—such as drinking too much alcohol or smoking—can put your health at risk.
- Try to eat right: It may help to have lunch with friends until you start having more of an interest in eating and cooking.
- Talk with caring friends: Let family and friends know when you want to talk about your parent. They may be grieving, too, and may welcome the chance to share memories. When possible, accept their offers of help and company.
- Visit with members of your religious community: Many people who are grieving find comfort in their faith. Praying, talking with others of faith, reading religious or spiritual texts, or listening to uplifting music also may bring comfort.

Stages of Grief

Elisabeth Kübler-Ross was a famous psychiatrist who pioneered the study of grief and developed five stages of grief that most people go through after the loss of a loved one.[1] People don't necessarily progress through these stages one by one but can move back and forth between stages at different times.

- Denial: Difficulty accepting that this has happened, in shock.
- Anger: Anger at yourself and/or God and life.

- Bargaining: Making deals with God and thinking about "if only" or "I should have" or "I could have."
- Depression: Loss, sadness, anxiety, emptiness.
- Acceptance: Starting to adjust and feeling a sense of hope.

Family and friends can be a great support, but sometimes people find grief counseling makes it easier to work through their sorrow. If you start feeling as if you need some assistance in working through some of these things, please consider finding help through the support of a professional counselor or a bereavement support group. It doesn't mean you are weak to ask for help. It actually means that you were strong enough to recognize that you needed some support. There are also support groups where grieving people help each other. You can check with religious groups, local hospitals, nursing homes, or your doctor to find a support group in your area.[2]

Your cultural beliefs, religion, prayer, meditation, and exercise can all be sources of support and comfort for you during this difficult time.

Grief during COVID-19

Grieving the loss of a loved one can be especially hard during COVID-19. Due to physical distancing guidelines, visiting a loved one at his or her end of life and people attending a funeral service may not be possible, depending on the guidelines in your state. It can also affect the ability of family and friends to come together in person and grieve in ways they might typically have done before the pandemic. The Centers for Disease Control offers information about actions you can take to help cope with loss and additional funeral guidance during COVID-19.[3]

PRACTICAL CONSIDERATIONS

This next section offers up some practical advice about the kinds of things that might need to be done after the loss of your parent, such as death certificates and other kinds of paperwork. As soon as possible, after the loss of your parent, the death must be officially pronounced by someone in authority like a doctor in a hospital or nursing facility or a hospice nurse. This person fills out the forms certifying the cause, time, and place of death. These steps will make it possible for an official death certificate to be prepared. This legal form is necessary for many reasons, including life insurance and financial and property issues.[4]

Over the next few weeks, you will want to notify a few organizations about your loved one's death. Here is a helpful list:

- The Social Security Administration: If the deceased was receiving Social Security benefits, you need to stop the checks.
- Life insurance companies: You will need a death certificate and policy numbers to make claims on any policies.
- Credit agencies: To prevent identity theft, you will want to send copies of the death certificate to three major firms: Equifax, Experian, and TransUnion.
- Banks and financial institutions: If your loved one left a list of accounts and passwords, it will be much easier to close or change accounts. You will need a copy of the death certificate if the person did not leave a list.

Chapter Fifteen

Questions to Consider

This chapter is your own personal space to write down some ideas, resources, services, goals, thoughts, and things to try out now or in the future. Consider this your place to actually write down what you may have already been thinking about and a place to get your thoughts organized. You are so busy with so many other things, and sometimes you just need one spot to jot down your private thoughts. I hope you find it helpful.

What ideas am I going to try?

What resources am I going to consider checking into?
For myself?

For my parent?

What services do I think could be helpful to us?

What questions do I have for my parent's doctor?

What are some end-of-life wishes/information that my parent has identified that I need to honor?

What kinds of things would help alleviate some of the strain I am feeling?

What problems do I want to address?

What questions do I still have?

What are my concerns?

What things can I do in the next few weeks to improve my situation (e.g., join a support group on Facebook)?

What things can I do over the long term to improve my situation (e.g., begin doing some financial planning or estate planning with my parent)?

What are some things I can do to start taking better care of myself?

What goals do I want to work on—for myself and/or my parent?

Table 15.1 has a template to help you start your list.

Table 15.1. The Caregiver's Lifeline

Resources/Supports/Agency	Phone Number	Website Address
Eldercare Locator	1-800-677-1116	https://eldercare.acl.gov

Notes

CHAPTER 1: DISAPPROVAL AND DISAPPOINTMENT VERSUS APPRECIATION AND RESPECT

1. E. C. Clipp and L. K. George, "Caregiver Needs and Patterns of Social Support," *Journal of Gerontology* 3 (1990): S102–11.

2. M. P. Lawton, M. H. Kleban, M. Moss, M. Rovine, and A. Glicksman, "Measuring Caregiving Appraisal," *Journal of Gerontology* 44 (1989): 61–71; Jennifer M. Kinney and Mary Ann Paris Stephens, "Hassles and Uplifts of Giving Care to a Family Member with Dementia," *Psychology and Aging* 4, no. 4 (1989): 402–8.

3. Alexis J. Walker and Katherine R. Allen, "Relationships between Caregiving Daughters and Their Elderly Mothers," *Gerontologist* 31 (1991): 389–96.

CHAPTER 2: SELF-FOCUSED THINKING VERSUS SELFLESS CONCERN

1. M. E. Hartford and R. Parsons, "Groups with Relatives or Dependent Older Adults," *Gerontologist* 22 (1982): 393–98.

2. Eleanor P. Stoller, "Elder-Caregiver Relationships in Shared Households," *Research on Aging* 7 (1985): 145–93; Elizabeth S. Johnson and Barbara J. Bursk, "Relationships between the Elderly and Their Adult Children," *Gerontologist* 17 (1983): 90–96.

3. N. L. Chappell, "Aging and Social Care," in *Handbook of Aging and the Social Sciences*, ed. R. H. Binstock and L. K. George (San Diego, CA: Academic Press, 1990), 438–54; L. K. George and L. P. Gwyther, "Caregivers Well-Being: A Multi-dimensional Examination of Family Caregivers of Demented Adults," *Gerontologist* 25 (1986): 253–59.

4. M. R. Haug, "Home Care for All Ill Elderly—Who Benefits?" *American Journal of Public Health* 25 (1985): 127–28.

5. E. Abel, "Adult Daughters and Care for the Elderly," *Feminist Studies* 12 (1986): 479–97; D. T. Reece and H. Hageboeck, "Intergenerational Care Providers of Noninstitutionalized Frail Elderly: Characteristics and Consequences," *Journal of Gerontological Social Work* 5 (1983): 21–34.

CHAPTER 3: PERSONAL PERFECTION VERSUS PERSONAL CONNECTION

1. Jennifer M. Kinney and Mary Ann Paris Stephens, "Hassles and Uplifts of Giving Care to a Family Member with Dementia," *Psychology and Aging* 4, no. 4 (1989): 402–8.

CHAPTER 4: EMOTIONAL INTERFERENCE VERSUS PERSONAL FULFILLMENT

1. S. K. Steinmetz, "Dependency, Stress, and Violence between Middle-Aged Caregivers and Their Elderly Parents," in *Abuse and Maltreatment of the Elderly: Causes and Interventions*, ed. J. Kosberg (Boston: John Wright, 1983), 134–49.

2. E. C. Clipp and L. K. George, "Caregiver Needs and Patterns of Social Support," *Journal of Gerontology* 3 (1990): S102–11.

3. Elaine M. Brody, "Parent Care as a Normative Family Stress," *Gerontologist* 25 (1985): 19–29.

4. Allan Horowitz, "Family, Kin and Friend Networks in Psychiatric Help-seeking," *Social Science & Medicine* 12 (1978): 297–304.

CHAPTER 5: A GENUINE VALUING OF THE MOTHER/ DAUGHTER RELATIONSHIP

1. Elizabeth S. Johnson and Barbara J. Bursk, "Relationships between the Elderly and Their Adult Children," *Gerontologist* 17 (1983): 90–96.

2. Alexis J. Walker, Sally S. K. Martin, and Laura L. Jones, "The Benefits and Costs of Caregiving and Care Receiving for Daughters and Mothers," *Journal of Gerontology* 3 (1992): S130–39.

3. Alexis J. Walker and Katherine R. Allen, "Relationships between Caregiving Daughters and Their Elderly Mothers," *Gerontologist* 31 (1991): 389–96.

4. Gary R. Lee and Eugene Ellithorpe, "Subjective Well-Being among the Elderly," *Journal of Marriage and the Family* 45 (1982): 457–65.

5. Charles H. Mindel and Roosevelt Wright, "Satisfaction in Multigenerational Households," *Journal of Gerontology* 37 (1982): 483–89.

CHAPTER 7: REALISTIC CONSIDERATIONS ABOUT LIVING TOGETHER

1. L. R. Fisher and C. Hoffman, "Who Cares for the Elderly: The Dilemma of Family Support," *Research in Social Problems and Public Policy* 3 (1984): 169–217.

2. Eleanor P. Stoller and Karen L. Pugliesi, "Other Roles of Caregivers: Competing Responsibilities for Supportive Resources," *Journal of Gerontology* 44 (1989): 231–38.

3. L. K. George and L. P. Gwyther, "Caregivers Well-Being: A Multi-dimensional Examination of Family Caregivers of Demented Adults," *Gerontologist* 25 (1986): 253–59.

4. Charles H. Mindel and Roosevelt Wright, "Satisfaction in Multigenerational Households," *Journal of Gerontology* 37 (1982): 483–89.

5. National Institute on Aging, "When It's Time to Leave Home," https://www.nia.nih.gov/health/when-its-time-leave-home.

CHAPTER 9: INHERITING MEMORIES

1. Social Care Institute for Excellence, "Reminiscence for People with Dementia," https://www.scie.org.uk/dementia/living-with-dementia/keeping-active/reminiscence.asp.

2. National Institute on Aging, "Tips for Improving Communication with Older Patients," https://www.nia.nih.gov/health/tips-improving-communication-older-patients/.

CHAPTER 10: HANDLING MEMORY LOSS

1. National Institute on Aging, "Do Memory Problems Always Mean Alzheimer's Disease?" https://www.nia.nih.gov/health/do-memory-problems -always-mean-alzheimers-disease.

2. National Institute on Mental Illness, "Depression," https://www.nami .org/About-Mental-Illness/mental-health-conditions/depression/overview (see the article's subheading "Warning Signs and Symptoms").

3. National Institute on Aging, "Depression and Older Adults," https:// www.nia.nih.gov/health/depression-and-older-adults.

4. National Institute on Aging, "Noticing Memory Problems and What to Do Next," https://www.nia.nih.gov/health/noticing-memory-problems-what -do-next/.

5. National Institute on Aging, "Alzheimer's Caregiving: Changes in Communication Skills," https://www.nia.nih.gov/health/alzheimers-caregiving -changes-communication-skills.

CHAPTER 11: THE CARE AND MAINTENANCE
OF THE CAREGIVER—*YOU!*

1. S. K. Steinmetz, "Dependency, Stress, and Violence between Middle-Aged Caregivers and Their Elderly Parents," in *Abuse and Maltreatment of the Elderly: Causes and Interventions*, ed. J. Kosberg (Boston: John Wright, 1983), 134–49.

2. Charles H. Mindel, "Multigenerational Family Households: Recent Trends and Implications for the Future," *Journal of Gerontology* 19 (1979): 456–63.

3. National Alliance for Caregiving and AARP, "Caregiving in the U.S.," June 2015, https:www.aarp.org/content/dam/aarp/ppi/2015/caregiving-in-the -united-states-2015-report-revised.pdf.

4. L. S. Noelker and D. M. Bass, "Home Care for the Elderly Persons: Linkages between Formal and Informal Caregivers," *Journal of Gerontology* 44 (1989): 536–70.

5. L. K. George and L. P. Gwyther, "Caregivers Well-Being: A Multi-dimensional Examination of Family Caregivers of Demented Adults," *Gerontologist* 25 (1986): 253–59.

6. Older Women's League, *Failing America's Caregivers: A Status Report on Women Who Care* (Washington, DC: OWL, 1989).

7. E. C. Clipp and L. K. George, "Caregiver Needs and Patterns of Social Support," *Journal of Gerontology* 3 (1990): S102–11.

8. Eleanor P. Stoller, "Elder-Caregiver Relationships in Shared Households," *Research on Aging* 7 (1985): 145–93.

9. N. L. Chappell, "Aging and Social Care," in *Handbook of Aging and the Social Sciences*, ed. R. H. Binstock and L. K. George (San Diego, CA: Academic Press, 1990), 438–54.

10. Mindel, "Multigenerational Family Households."

11. R. J. V. Montgomery and E. F. Borgatta, "The Effects of Alternative Supportive Strategies on Family Caregiving," *Gerontologist* 29 (1989): 457–64.

12. Patricia Archbold, "Impact of Parent Caring on Women," *Family Relations* 52 (1983): 39–45; Elaine M. Brody, "Parent Care as a Normative Family Stress," *Gerontologist* 25 (1985): 19–29; M. H. Cantor, "The Informal Support System: Its Relevance in the Lives of the Elderly," in *Aging and Society*, ed. E. Borgatta and N. McCluskey (Beverly Hills, CA: Sage, 1980), 131–47.

13. M. E. Hartford and R. Parsons, "Groups with Relatives or Dependent Older Adults," *Gerontologist* 22 (1982): 396.

14. Clipp and George, "Caregiver Needs and Patterns of Social Support."

CHAPTER 12: DEALING WITH DIFFICULT BEHAVIORS

1. Marlo Sollitto, "Dealing with an Elderly Parent's Difficult Behavior," AgingCare.com, November 20, 2020, https://www.agingcare.com/articles/how-to-handle-an-elderly-parents-bad-behavior-138673.htm.

CHAPTER 13: NAVIGATING THE SYSTEM

1. Steven Abel, "Social Security Retirement Benefits: The Last Insult of a Sexist Society," *Family Court Review* 36, no. 1 (1998): 55–64.

2. Richard Johnson and Claire Xiaozhi Wang, "The Financial Burden of Paid Home Health Care on Older Adults: Oldest and Sickest Are Least Likely to Have Income," *Health Affairs* 38 (2019): 994–1002.

3. National Institute on Aging, "Long Distance Caregiving," https://www.nia.nih.gov.health/caregiving/long-distance-caregiving.

4. Sindya Bhanoo, "Pandemic Forces Family Members into New Role," *Washington Post*, March 23, 2020.

5. US Bureau of Labor Statistics, "Unpaid Eldercare in the United States 2017–2018," November 22, 2019, https://www.bls.gov/news.release/elcare.nr0.htm.

CHAPTER 14: LIFE AFTER CAREGIVING: NOW WHAT?

1. Elisabeth Kübler-Ross, *On Death and Dying* (New York: Macmillan, 1969).
2. National Institute on Aging, "Mourning the Death of a Spouse," https://www.nia.nih.gov/health/mourning-death-spouse#what.
3. Centers for Disease Control, "Funeral Guidance," https://www.cdc/gov/coronavirus/2019-ncov/daily-life-coping/funeral-guidance.html.
4. National Institute on Aging, "What to Do after Someone Dies," https://www.nia.nih.gov/health/what-do-after-someone-dies/.

Bibliography

Abel, E. "Adult Daughters and Care for the Elderly." *Feminist Studies* 12 (1986): 479–97.

Abel, Steven. "Social Security Retirement Benefits: The Last Insult of a Sexist Society." *Family Court Review* 36, no. 1 (1998): 55–64.

AgingCare. "Connecting Families with Elder Care, Senior Housing Caregiver Support." https://www.agingcare.com/.

Archbold, Patricia. "Impact of Parent Caring on Women." *Family Relations* 52 (1983): 39–45.

Bhanoo, Sindya. "Pandemic Forces Family Members into New Role." *Washington Post*, March 23, 2020.

Brody, Elaine M. "Parent Care as a Normative Family Stress." *Gerontologist* 25 (1985): 19–29.

Cantor, M. H. "The Informal Support System: Its Relevance in the Lives of the Elderly." In *Aging and Society*, edited by E. Borgatta and N. McCluskey, 131–47. Beverly Hills, CA: Sage, 1980.

Centers for Disease Control. "Funeral Guidance." https://www.cdc/gov/coronavirus/2019-ncov/daily-life-coping/funeral-guidance.html.

Chappell, N. L. "Aging and Social Care." In *Handbook of Aging and the Social Sciences*, edited by R. H. Binstock and L. K. George, 438–54. San Diego, CA: Academic Press, 1990.

Clipp, E. C., and L. K. George. "Caregiver Needs and Patterns of Social Support." *Journal of Gerontology* 3 (1990): S102–11.

Fisher, L. R., and C. Hoffman. "Who Cares for the Elderly: The Dilemma of Family Support." *Research in Social Problems and Public Policy* 3 (1984): 169–217.

George, L. K., and L. P. Gwyther. "Caregivers Well-Being: A Multi-dimensional Examination of Family Caregivers of Demented Adults." *Gerontologist* 25 (1986): 253–59.

Hartford, M. E., and R. Parsons. "Groups with Relatives or Dependent Older Adults." *Gerontologist* 22 (1982): 393–98.

Haug, M. R. "Home Care for All Ill Elderly—Who Benefits?" *American Journal of Public Health* 25 (1985): 127–28.

Horowitz, Allan. "Family, Kin and Friend Networks in Psychiatric Helpseeking." *Social Science & Medicine* 12 (1978): 297–304.

Johnson, Elizabeth S., and Barbara J. Bursk. "Relationships between the Elderly and Their Adult Children." *Gerontologist* 17 (1983): 90–96.

Johnson, Richard, and Claire Xiaozhi Wang. "The Financial Burden of Paid Home Health Care on Older Adults: Oldest and Sickest Are Least Likely to Have Income." *Health Affairs* 38 (2019): 994–1002.

Kinney, Jennifer M., and Mary Ann Paris Stephens. "Hassles and Uplifts of Giving Care to a Family Member with Dementia." *Psychology and Aging* 4, no. 4 (1989): 402–8.

Kübler-Ross, Elisabeth. *On Death and Dying.* New York: Macmillan, 1969.

Lawton, M. P., M. H. Kleban, M. Moss, M. Rovine, and A. Glicksman. "Measuring Caregiving Appraisal." *Journal of Gerontology* 44 (1989): 61–71.

Lee, Gary R., and Eugene Ellithorpe. "Subjective Well-Being among the Elderly." *Journal of Marriage and the Family* 45 (1982): 457–65.

Mindel, Charles H. "Multigenerational Family Households: Recent Trends and Implications for the Future." *Journal of Gerontology* 19 (1979): 456–63.

Mindel, Charles H., and Roosevelt Wright. "Satisfaction in Multigenerational Households." *Journal of Gerontology* 37 (1982): 483–89.

Montgomery, R. J. V., and E. F. Borgatta. "The Effects of Alternative Supportive Strategies on Family Caregiving." *Gerontologist* 29 (1989): 457–64.

National Alliance for Caregiving and AARP. "Caregiving in the U.S." June 2015. https:www.aarp.org/content/dam/aarp/ppi/2015/caregiving-in-the -united-states-2015-report-revised.pdf.

National Institute on Aging. "Alzheimer's Caregiving: Changes in Communication Skills." https://www.nia.nih.gov/health/alzheimers-caregiving -changes-communication-skills.

———. "Depression and Older Adults." https://www.nia.nih.gov/health /depression-and-older-adults.

———. "Do Memory Problems Always Mean Alzheimer's Disease?" https:// www.nia.nih.gov/health/do-memory-problems-always-mean-alzheimers -disease.

———. "Health Information." https://www.nia.nih.gov/health.

———. "Long Distance Caregiving." https://www.nia.nih.gov.health/caregiv ing/long-distance-caregiving.

———. "Mourning the Death of a Spouse." https://www.nia.nih.gov/health/mourning-death-spouse#what.

———. "Noticing Memory Problems and What to Do Next." https://www.nia.nih.gov/health/noticing-memory-problems-what-do-next.

———. "Tips for Improving Communication with Older Patients." https://www.nia.nih.gov/health/tips-improving-communication-older-patients/.

———. "What to Do after Someone Dies." https://www.nia.nih.gov/health/what-do-after-someone-dies/.

———. "When It's Time to Leave Home." https://www.nia.nih.gov/health/when-its-time-leave-home.

National Institute on Mental Illness. "Depression." https://www.nami.org/About-Mental-Illness/mental-health-conditions/depression/overview.

Noelker, L. S., and D. M. Bass. "Home Care for the Elderly Persons: Linkages between Formal and Informal Caregivers." *Journal of Gerontology* 44 (1989): 536–70.

Older Women's League. *Failing America's Caregivers: A Status Report on Women Who Care.* Washington, DC: OWL, 1989.

Reece, D. T., and H. Hageboeck. "Intergenerational Care Providers of Noninstitutionalized Frail Elderly: Characteristics and Consequences." *Journal of Gerontological Social Work* 5 (1983): 21–34.

Social Care Institute for Excellence. "Reminiscence for People with Dementia." https://www.scie.org.uk/dementia/living-with-dementia/keeping-active/reminiscence.asp.

Sollitto, Marlo. "Dealing with an Elderly Parent's Difficult Behavior." Aging Care.com, November 20, 2020. https://www.agingcare.com/articles/how-to-handle-an-elderly-parents-bad-behavior-138673.htm.

Steinmetz, S. K. "Dependency, Stress, and Violence between Middle-Aged Caregivers and Their Elderly Parents." In *Abuse and Maltreatment of the Elderly: Causes and Interventions*, edited by J. Kosberg, 134–49. Boston: John Wright, 1983.

Stoller, Eleanor P. "Elder-Caregiver Relationships in Shared Households." *Research on Aging* 7 (1985): 145–93.

Stoller, Eleanor P., and Karen L. Pugliesi. "Other Roles of Caregivers: Competing Responsibilities for Supportive Resources." *Journal of Gerontology* 44 (1989): 231–38.

US Bureau of Labor Statistics. "Unpaid Eldercare in the United States 2017–2018." November 22, 2019. https://www.bls.gov/news.release/elcare.nr0.htm.

Walker, Alexis J., and Katherine R. Allen. "Relationships between Caregiving Daughters and Their Elderly Mothers." *Gerontologist* 31 (1991): 389–96.

Walker, Alexis J., Sally S. K. Martin, and Laura L. Jones. "The Benefits and Costs of Caregiving and Care Receiving for Daughters and Mothers." *Journal of Gerontology* 3 (1992): S130–39.

Index

Page references for tables are italicized.

About the Author

Jeanne R. Lord, PhD, began her career with a senior citizens' nutrition program, followed by an appointment to the University of Illinois Cooperative Extension's Adult Life and Aging Team. In addition, she taught at Northern Illinois University. In 2000, Dr. Lord returned to her alma mater, Eastern Illinois University (EIU), where she is currently a professor in the Department of Human Services and Community Leadership. During her tenure at EIU, she has served as associate dean for ten years and then as interim dean for one year for the College of Health and Human Services. She has presented at numerous state, national, and international conferences and has published in professional journals. She has received university awards for teaching, research, service, and leadership.